TEENAGE
REBELLION

TEENAGE REBELLION

Truman E. Dollar

and

Grace H. Ketterman, M.D.

FLEMING H. REVELL COMPANY
OLD TAPPAN, NEW JERSEY

Scripture quotations are based on the King James Version of the Bible.

Lyrics from "The Cat's in the Cradle" by Harry and Sandy Chapin are reprinted by permission.

"Straight Talk Gets Shafted" from *American Flint,* published by Glassworkers Union of N. America, Toledo, Ohio. Used by permission.

Library of Congress Cataloging in Publication Data

Dollar, Truman.
   Teenage rebellion.

   Includes bibliographical references.
   1. Problem children.   2. Adolescent psychology.
3. Conflict of generations.   4. Parent and child.
5. United States—Social conditions—1945-
I. Ketterman, Grace H., joint author.   II. Title.
HQ773.D6   301.43'15   79-18957
ISBN 0-8007-1059-2

TO *Donna*

With appreciation for
her generosity and love

Contents

Preface

Admittedly, it is uncommon for a fundamental Baptist minister and a child psychiatrist to combine efforts to write about training children. Traditionally, they have been considered natural philosophical enemies. Their training and approaches to problem solving are dramatically dissimilar. It is, however, the conviction of the authors that the chief value of this book lies in the findings and contributions of two born-again believers with diverse backgrounds, who have mutual respect for each other and who are unalterably committed to scriptural authority. Dr. Grace H. Ketterman's experience embraces pediatric medicine and psychiatry. Rev. Truman E. Dollar's background includes, in addition to training in theology, a degree with a major in history and a minor in sociology.

Although the authors strongly believe in absolute biblical authority, they make no claim to agree on all matters of religious affiliation or on the subtle nuances of doctrine. However, there is perfect agreement on all fundamental doctrines.

In addition to fifty years of their combined experience in working with troubled young people, a detailed questionnaire was used to probe for information. One hundred young people were interviewed.

The questions were designed to evaluate the behavior, philosophy, and thought patterns of modern American youth. Those taking the survey were carefully chosen to represent every facet of teen life in the country. Throughout every section of the nation, young people with diverse backgrounds, religious and cultural, were included. Criminals, hard-drug users, honor students, Christian and unchristian, were questioned. Some interviews were held in prison cells; others in public schools and Christian schools of differing quality and philosophy. Every interview was personally conducted by Truman Dollar and took approximately fifty minutes.

Each child was shown a waiver signed by his parent or guardian which guaranteed complete confidentiality and anonymity. He was assured that the questions would be discontinued immediately upon his request. Not one young person refused to answer a question. Each teen surveyed, when asked, responded that the interview was both fair and significant. A copy of the parental consent form reads as follows:

> I hereby give consent for my child to be interviewed by Rev. Truman Dollar. I understand that the survey is designed to determine the cause of rebellion and its cure. It is clear to me that the survey does not imply that my child is necessarily rebellious.
>
> I also understand that, in the interest of candor, I will not be shown the individual responses of my child.

Certain basic presumptions were used in the interviews. They arose out of the biblical and philosophical backgrounds of the authors. It seemed essential to the authors to include those presumptions in the introduction to allow the reader to view the authors' approach. They follow:

1. The Bible states the principles that cause or avoid rebellion.
2. Surveys of rebellious children do not establish truth; they can only explain or illustrate it.
3. There is a direct relationship between the life-style, actions, and attitudes of the parents, and the values and theology of the children.
4. Rebellious children rarely, if ever, perceive that their values and theology result from reaction to their parents. Rebellious children will generally attribute their attitudes to their own independent thought processes. Each considers his situation unique.
5. There are common denominators among rebellious children.
6. An effective survey will provide an explanation for families in which one child rebels and the others do not.

7. An effective survey will help parents of moldable children do a better job in training their offspring.

8. Rebellion is avoidable, not genetic; and not the result of natural personality qualities. Man's sinful nature is the basic cause.

9. Definition of rebellion: either a conscious or unconscious rejection of the values, life-style, and/or theology of one's parents.

Although the authors believed the survey would confirm some conclusions already made, some totally unexpected trends were uncovered. Some of the answers dramatically altered the understanding and approach to dealing with youth problems. The interviews will be relied upon heavily throughout the book for verification, illustration, and insights gained by the authors. A copy of the survey and the answers are included in the appendix of the book.

The anonymity of all those interviewed as well as counselees must be protected to maintain both their privacy and the authors' professional integrity. It is with that in mind that the names used in illustrations and case studies have been changed or the persons otherwise disguised.

Foreword

During the past twenty-five years more books have been written on how to raise good children than in the whole of previous history. The reason for this increase is because child raising is more difficult today than ever before. There are more enemy forces both within and outside the home than have ever existed. Parenthood has become a very complex task. Fortunately these new books on child rearing are coming along at an ideal time.

Teenage Rebellion makes a positive contribution to the field with a unique approach. Dr. Grace Ketterman, a child psychiatrist, and Reverend Truman Dollar, a Bible-believing minister, are the first people I know of who researched one hundred teenagers personally to examine the true causes of their rebellion and present·a sane, biblically faithful solution. Too many writers today discuss problems at great length, but come up with very little in the way of remedies. These authors did not make that mistake, for two-thirds of the book offers sound solutions to the enormous problem of teenage rebellion. I have observed too many books either fail to understand the *cause* of the problem or they suggest unbiblical solutions. These authors did neither.

In fact, I was pleased in reading the manuscript to find that they placed the responsibility for raising good children primarily on the father and then on the mother. Both parents are given some very positive instructions on what to do to avoid raising teenage rebels. They even include some fine suggestions for those parents whose teens are already rebellious—they need help too.

There is no greater influence in the life of a child than his mother, father, and schoolteacher. The school should be thought of, not as a replacement for parental training, but as a supplement to it.

Speaking of influence on children, I have found it follows this basic overlapping pattern: from birth to three years—mother; from three to six years—mother and father; from six to eighteen years—father; from seven to thirteen years—teacher (teens, peer group).

Many parents do not take advantage of their enormous opportunity for training their children because they do not fully realize the extent of their influence. Other parents just don't know what to do—and still others don't care. This book cannot help the last group, but parents who care will be greatly helped.

Through the years I have observed that the two biggest mistakes parents make are: (1) not spending the necessary time with their children to be the kind of parents they should be, and (2) letting their teens select their own friends. Even good parenting in younger years can be negated by the wrong kind of friends later on. First Corinthians 15:53 warns against evil companions who corrupt good morals. The problem with being a parent is that we all start out as amateurs. If you feel insecure or inadequate for your task—join the club. The answer is not to adopt your children (although that may seem tempting sometimes), nor is it to refuse having children. The answer is to become a self-taught expert as a parent and that will come primarily by reading the Bible and good books on parenting. This book is one all parents should include in their curriculum. And it isn't just parents of teenagers who should read it. The time to avoid raising teenage rebels is when they're young—when mother and dad have so much influence on them.

It isn't as easy to raise good children as it once was, but we do have better helps. This book will help you avoid the mistakes many well-meaning parents have made, and someday you will see its benefits in your most treasured possession—your children.

Tim LaHaye, Pastor
Scott Memorial Baptist Church

Acknowledgments

Acknowledgments are not frequently read, but they should be. Every author understands that no significant book can be written without the help and encouragement of others.

The authors wish to thank Dr. Tim LaHaye for reading the manuscript, for his suggestions, and for his encouragement.

A research committee of three women worked for over a year locating specific articles and books, maintaining a massive filing system, and noting materials which the authors quoted. Donna Oman was Chairman and Pat Peterson and Sue Roehr worked tirelessly. Sue Roehr read hundreds of articles in compiling the necessary data and read the manuscript and made corrections.

Dr. Herbert Ketterman patiently took time from his busy medical practice to critique several chapters. His input was most valuable.

Bonnie Johnson, Ann Kistler, Donna Oman, Charlotte Franklin, and Larry Franklin helped compile the results of the teen interviews. Clarissa Loper completed calculations to bring order to the final draft of the survey.

Kay Kimes typed initial drafts of some chapters. Clarissa Loper typed and retyped the entire book during the eighteen months of research. Mrs. Loper also proofed the final draft of the manuscript and checked all source notes. Her contribution to the book cannot be overstated.

Introduction

A brief historical and analytical summary of modern psychology seems essential. It is especially important as it relates to its philosophical foundations and the theological biases of the authors. This obvious conflict must be highlighted at the very outset for this book to be understood.

Modern psychology had its beginning in the late nineteenth century with the work of Sigmund Freud. Although he is considered to be the father of present-day psychiatry, his students and other behavioral scientists emerged quickly as research broadened. Abruptly, the study of the mind became a serious discipline. Ignored at first by the general public and most medical people, Freud's methods spread because he developed techniques to treat mental illness previously thought to be a hopeless disorder.

Unfortunately, Freud believed that a personal God was only a myth. He viewed all religion as ''a device to control bad behavior,'' and called it the ''universal neurosis.'' Freud's theology is not uncommon among today's psychiatrists. The reader, however, will be benefited by a summary of the approaches of some major figures in this field of study.

From the outset of psychological studies, various schools of thought developed. Their means of access to the understanding and treatment of mental illnesses differed widely. After a century, the divisions continue, and the mental-health field is fragmented into as many camps as the religious cultists.

Freud's students are familiar: Alfred Adler, Carl Jung, and Freud's own daughter, Anna. Their work was based on lengthy analyses of their patients' early life experiences, with the interpretation of the influence of such events on adult feelings and problems. A process like this was laborious, lengthy, immensely expensive, and limited to a relatively few people.

About the same time, Ivan Pavlov, a Russian, began studying animals and discovered the interaction of behavior and environment. Pavlov believed that behavior is simply a conditioned reflex and demonstrated that animals could be trained to a high degree of conformity to the trainer's demands. This humanistic approach extended in his studies to people as well. He opened the door to understanding a feelingless and impersonal society. Several current books such as *Future Shock* explain the social development.

Max Wertheimer combined some of the ideas of Freud and Pavlov and in the early 1900s introduced *Gestaltism*. He taught the need to see life as a whole, integrating all conscious experiences as important along with physical forces. Gestalt techniques are enjoying a modern-day revival in an attempt to help the neurotic patient reintegrate the fragments of a shattered personality.

A major reemphasis is growing today on behavior modification. Based on the original studies of Pavlov, John Watson, and others have taught that it is what people do that determines how they feel rather than the reverse. The answer to problems, they argue, rests not on the past nor on the feelings, but simply on behavior. By setting up a series of positive or adverse consequences, behavior can be molded according to the values or will of the therapist. Behavior modification is widely accepted today among practicing therapists. Modern behaviorism totally ignores the spiritual part of man.

Since 1950, a flood of books and philosophies has emerged based on Dr. Eric Berne's work. Dr. Berne, a Freudian psychoanalyst, redefined the old personality description (ego, superego, and id) into lay language. His terms, for example, the parent, adult, and child ego states, have freed the mental-health world from technical terms and translated them into simple language even children can understand.

Dr. Eric Erickson, Melanie Klein, Jean Piaget, Abraham Maslow, and many others have researched the field of developmental psychology and have emphasized the basic needs and feelings of children as being fundamental to well-adjusted adult life.

Dr. Thomas Harris, Muriel James, William Glasser, and Thomas Gordon have become household words. They have devoted their studies to understanding, curing, and preventing mental and emotional illnesses. And yet, today there is more illness, with its painful varieties of expression, than when these studies began. It seems clear that the explosion of the study of mental illness that rejects a biblical framework does not work.

At a recent nationwide psychiatric convention, there was a refreshing awareness in some papers for the need of a spiritual emphasis and a "permission" to invite patients to explore this area of their lives. There is a need for this consciousness to grow.

Hundreds of books have been written by psychiatrists about child training which have rejected or ignored the Bible. The result has been a part of the great twentieth-century American tragedy. Ministers have written books about child rearing focusing upon spiritual principles. Now spiritual principles must always underlie and dictate life's answers, but ministers have all too frequently ignored the whole story. History, morally neutral psychological studies, and cultural trends have for the most part been absent from the writings of spiritual leaders. It is the plan of the authors of this book to relate biblical principles and sound psychological techniques as they apply to modern America's problems.

It is true that the Bible always has the answer, but case studies and history illustrate scriptural truth. It is also true that although Freud, Pavlov, Ericson, and Spock were humanists, they did make some valid observations and develop some workable techniques. These men also developed some philosophies that others used to their spiritual destruction, adversely affecting our entire culture. Man is not a genetic accident; he is the design of God. He is also not simply the product of his environment. Man is a moral, rational, emotional, and spiritual being. He must be considered in that total framework. The authors totally reject the humanist position and strongly believe that man must be considered as a spiritual being, accountable to God, or the observations and conclusions will not be sound. In order to deliver society from the disaster of anti-God philosophies of psychological studies, the research needs to include spiritual values.

Conservative Christians have learned to be wary of psychiatry. And small wonder! Most of the above people have ignored or ridiculed the existence and impact of a personal God upon human experience.

Evangelical theologians have, on the other hand, written and taught honestly the power of prayer and Scripture, but many have failed to see the valid intermingling of the seeds of truth in good psychology with the eternal truth of God's Word. A patient of one of the authors once said, "I see that I took my neurosis into my new Christian faith and read in the Bible only those ideas that fit my problems. I didn't see the positive, victorious verses, only the laborious, negative ones."

Sifting out sound and useful ideas from many researchers and relating them to basic historic Christian teachings is needed today. To deny the validity of many of those studies is intellectually dishonest. To fail to test them against the truth of God's Word is spiritually dangerous.

This book is an attempt to examine, in a restricted area, psychological and biblical truths and to study one in the light of the other, honestly and fearlessly.

Chapter 1

The Runaway American

"Pastor, I wish my father was dead!"

The son of a prominent midwestern theologian sat in my office listening with a cynical smile while I talked and probed. He was cocky and knew that I was keenly aware of his attitude.

I had just asked, "If you could change one thing about your father, what would it be?" The quick response was an outburst of anger, hatred, and frustration against his dad.

I felt certain his bitter response was calculated, at least partially, for its shock value as well as grasping at an opportunity to discredit his father in my presence. It was another way to strike out against the one he blamed for his problems.

A disheveled, jeans-clad, sixteen-year-old girl sat handcuffed to a chair in one of our pastoral offices. The metal restrainers were not my idea, and emotionally I resisted the whole approach. I sat across the desk while she leaned her head on her free hand. Her relaxed jaw distorted her facial expression. There was no fear, but she seethed with hate. Although she came from a proper, middle-class home, her dirty fingernails and unwashed hair suggested she was totally unconcerned about personal hygiene or appearance.

In less than thirty minutes, her father would arrive and, along with one of the youth ministers from the church I pastor, would escort her to Corpus Christi, Texas. There she would be detained against her will for many months in a home for incorrigible girls.

I had been given permission to interview her if she agreed to cooperate. "Why do you run away?" I asked.

"I hate my father. He has been married many times, and he doesn't love me." She answered my questions, but obviously used every opportunity to discredit her father.

I learned that later that day, when airline officials refused to let her aboard the plane in handcuffs, she escaped again briefly. A chase took place in full view of curious Kansas City travelers and ended abruptly when she was literally tackled and brought under control. She had looked like a running back fleeing a linebacker. Safely on board the plane, she stoically accepted her fate. She was legally committed later that day by troubled, but relieved, parents to an institution they knew only by reputation. They had already exhausted every means available to control the girl's behavior.

I sat in my office at the mental-health center, listening to a father tell his shocking story. I felt a trace of strain, as he described the severe condition of his child.

Outside the door, with her puppy, sat Linda, his twelve-year-old daughter. She was so severely withdrawn that she could not relate to people, only animals. She was the only child we ever admitted with a pet.

The family had just returned from an extended vacation, where, without warning, the daughter had tried to push her father down an abandoned mine shaft. The distraught parents were pleading for help. They had not a clue to explain her behavior or emotional withdrawal. Painfully, they had been witnessing her slow retreat, but had done nothing until her recent climactic attempt to kill her father.

In our counseling sessions and alone, Linda slowly opened up over the weeks we spent together. An eleven-year-old school friend had been stricken with leukemia. It was a long, lingering illness. "She looked so pale and weak. I was worried and scared," she said sincerely. When her friend died, it was unusually traumatic for the child. Her grief was very real.

The parents had misread the depth of that grief. "It was not even your best friend," they reasoned. To Linda it was the ultimate put-down. Her parents could not understand, so she ran away to her own little world of puppies, kittens, and horses.

The phone at our home rang late at night. An executive of one of America's largest publishers of Bibles and religious books was on the phone. "Truman, I need help. My sixteen-year-old daughter has been gone from home for a month." He explained that she was on drugs and drank heavily, and that she was living with several other runaways in a large, nearby, southern city. He knew where she was, but believed it was futile to bring her home forcibly. "She would just run away again," he reasoned. He wanted his daughter, not her mere physical presence.

He asked for my advice and help in getting her rehabilitated. His mood was one of total despair.

Later that week he took a leave of absence from his work and drove his daughter eight-hundred miles to a coastal city where he committed her to a home for girls. The entire drive was in hostile silence, and she was guarded every mile of the trip like a dangerous criminal.

A bright and articulate seventeen-year-old boy sat in my office pouring out his soul. Initially, he had come with great reservation, but, after only ten minutes, he was unloading his pent-up feelings. It had taken less prompting than I ever imagined for him to talk.

"On my eighteenth birthday I plan to go to school as usual, pack all my belongings, and walk out." He was referring to a Christian school where he had been enrolled against his will. He then explained that he intended to drive to the local public high school and enroll himself. There he would complete his senior year.

During a runaway the previous summer, he had learned that his legal rights were fragile at best. It was because of that ordeal that he decided to wait. However, on the very day he obtained his legal rights as an adult, he would make his move. His parents were totally unaware of his intentions and expressed gratitude for the change they had recently begun to notice in their rebellious son. They misinterpreted his conformity as a change of heart.

The relationship between Sherry and her parents had steadily deteriorated during the past three years. It seemed, at least to this sixteen-year-old, that she simply could not please them. Her hair was too long, her study habits too short, and they were "on her back" most of the time. The problems became so severe that the parents wanted professional help. I was still involved in private practice at the time, so regular counseling sessions were begun. They had waited too long, however, and the pressures were too intense.

One morning in October, Sherry failed to appear at breakfast. There was no note, no message, not a clue. In fact, despite desperate searching, days passed, but she could not be found.

After three painful weeks, the frantic parents finally discovered their daughter in the basement of the house next door. A misguided thirty-year-old divorcée had hidden the girl during the search. Her attempts at help included introducing the teenager to marijuana and alcohol.

The girl believed she had made her point. She had proved she was smart—smarter than her parents. She ran, and far away, but never even left the neighborhood.

The relieved father explained that the brain tumor just removed was three inches in diameter. His daughter was still not completely out of danger, but his mood was joyous. After the mother learned that hearing was permanently lost in one ear, she smiled through her tears and said, "I still have my baby."

It had been only three weeks since the father brought his sixteen-year-old daughter to my office for an interview pursuant to this book. He vaguely knew something was wrong and suggested he had failed as a father.

He hoped for answers that might reveal what he and his wife had to do to reverse the anxieties and the social and emotional withdrawal of their daughter.

After fifty minutes of questions and halting, tearful answers, I asked the girl if she would like her pastor to help. She quickly responded, and with her face buried in her hands and sobbing uncontrollably, nodded her head.

I talked with both parents immediately. This was no failure of the home. There *was* something wrong, and this girl needed help. They gratefully accepted my offer, although fearful of what they would learn, and gave me a free hand.

Quickly, I talked to my colleague and coauthor of this book. "Grace, I know you run a home for girls and are not in a private practice, but I need your help." Over the phone I explained the symptoms and family history. I speculated there was a serious neurological problem. She agreed and arranged for an evaluation at the Kansas University Medical Center. It was two weeks before an appointment could be made.

The doctors examined her externally on Monday and operated on Friday, removing a tumor that had been lodged on her brain for years. Only recently had it begun to grow to immense proportions.

Judy did not run away, but her body took her away for a while. She has now returned, whole, to thankful parents.

There she sat; small, statuesque, silhouetted against the mountains of Vail, Colorado. Her back was stiff and her deeply tanned legs crossed in the classic yoga position for meditation. In her hands were tiny beads to keep tally of her Buddhist prayers. Although shade and a soft grass mound were nearby, she had purposely positioned herself, motionless, elevated on a hard wooden ledge. Her frayed jeans were cut short, a sleeveless sweater exposed her arms to the afternoon sun. Exotic beads ringed her neck, and a curious little wool hat covered just the top of her tied-back hair.

Suddenly she relaxed, uncrossed her legs, put her beads away and reclined, oblivious of the passersby. I asked my wife to walk ahead while I stopped to converse. The temptation to probe her mind was irresistible. She was quiet, easy to talk to. When I told her I was coauthoring a book on the causes of rebellion, she was eager to answer my questions. It was clear she had hoped to learn as much from me as I did from her. Her searching for answers to her own behavior was only thinly veiled.

It had all started nine years ago when she left home for her freshman year in college. She returned after the first year to her conservative Mennonite family, a different person, committed to Eastern mysticism and travel. After nine years, she was still searching and had spent the past twelve months aimlessly roaming the country, sleeping at night in a tent.

I carefully but persistently probed the relationship with her parents and conflicts over theology and life-style. She insisted there were no conflicts and was quick to assure me that at least twice each year she visted her parents. Her unusually strong emphasis on these issues suggested to me that they were painful.

When I called attention to the obvious conflicts between Buddhism and a personal commitment to Christ as the redemptive Son of God, she showed signs of discomfort. "I still believe what my parents do, I just understand Christ's love and purpose better than they do." Emotionally, she could not bring herself, even after almost a decade of wandering, to admit she had run away theologically.

 It began on a snowy Monday morning in January. I had been earnestly studying alone in my upstairs office at home. It was the kind of day that busy ministers need for study and meditation. The heavy snow relieved the pressure of other pastoral responsibilities, and I was surrounded with books and isolation. I had instructed my secretary not to refer any calls that would disrupt my total concentration unless there was an emergency.

I reached instinctively for the phone when it rang, but with some irritation at interruption. "Please call the Workmans' immediately. There is some serious problem." I clicked the receiver and dialed the number I had been given. My mood quickly changed. These people never called unless there was a real need.

Marvin Workman, a professional man and member of our church, answered the phone. Abruptly he said, "Truman, Nathan is dead. He shot himself. Can you come?" My stomach knotted. I was stunned. My response was brief and a bit confused. Moments later I was racing across the city. I had a little time to think. He was only nineteen, and I had known him since he was in kindergarten. Only four months before he sat in my office, his parents just outside the door, and told me he had come to believe there was no God. He was quiet, honest, and conversation was easy. He politely accepted my gift of the book by Josh McDowell, *Evidence That Demands a Verdict*. It was later returned unread.

I quietly pleaded with a grieved father not to go outside. He paced back and forth across the room unaware of his actions, almost totally out of control. "Remember him when he was alive," I suggested again. The father insisted, however, and asked again for me to go with him. Reluctantly, I opened the patio door, and we walked out in the cold onto the elevated wooden deck. It had been shoveled, but scattered snow thinly covered some areas.

A few feet to the right were steps that led down to the snow-covered backyard. I first saw his feet, then the rest of his frozen body. His hands were still cradled around the 20-gauge shotgun. At the top of the steps his father dropped on one knee, his face covered with his hands. He almost looked as though he was kneeling to pray. Over my shoulder I heard him say, "I've killed my son." Haltingly, he made his way to the grotesque figure on the ground. He fell across the body. Now sobbing, he talked as if the body could hear: "Nathan, I loved you so much." His hands lovingly fingered his son's coat around his chest and neck. "I'll never see you again." He wanted to remain, and his desire was unchanged by the gruesome scene.

I pleaded with the father to return to the family room. It seemed like an eternity, and I was utterly helpless to say or do anything to comfort. The father and I had been intimate friends for twenty years, but everything I considered saying seemed absurd. I wanted to run, and only my responsibility as a pastor kept me there.

My thoughts raced back to the night before, when the family had left for church while he watched Dallas beating Denver in the Super Bowl. Intellectually, I knew a lifeless body felt no pain. Emotionally, I had mental images of the family returning from church unaware that less than twenty feet from where they ate a late night snack, his body lay; all night in the howling January wind and cold—he was motionless, gone. My imagination ran wild as I remembered the story of the dog being let out at 11:00 P.M. the night before.

Inside, a weeping mother, an eighteen-year-old brother, and a sixteen-year-old sister awaited our return. The guilt that always accompanies suicide was everywhere. The father blamed himself, while the others confessed their contributions to the tragedy. I sat quietly. This was not an occasion for sermons. There seemed to be nothing I could do but remain and listen.

In preparation for this book, I planned to interview one hundred young people; he was the first teen whose parents had given consent. The questions were still being refined, and I preached his funeral before they were typed.

Nathan, like all the others, had run away, but he would not be back.

There is a war going on between parents and children in this country and like all wars, it's hell. Its beginning has been marked by most in the early sixties. Millions of parents—especially Christian parents—are fearful either to admit the problem or to discuss it. It's like a family secret. Many mistakenly believe their family situation is unique. The truth is that it has become a national plague. The dimensions of the conflict are not fully known, but all the visible signs indicate that it is immense and escalating daily. Its shape continually varies; it is still in the process of evolution. The changing outward symptoms do not mean the problems are going away.

The history, the problem, the causes, the solutions need discussion. Let's start with the first most obvious symptom, the runaway

American. The runaways are only symptoms of larger, deeper problems. Like a mystical, historical cycle, one hundred years after the Civil War our nation was again plunged into a turbulent era. Only this time our national fabric was cut into a million pieces rather than two. It was not the North against the South, but father against son and daughter against mother. Traditional social institutions including civil authority, marriage, and the family were severely threatened.

The sixties was a pivotal decade, every bit as dramatic as its counterpart in the previous century. It was a frightening, historical era. The drama is not over yet, only the characters and mood have changed.

It was an age of technological revolution; a knowledge explosion. Space travel became a reality, and the computer touched everything. Biochemists tinkered with the genetic code, and nuclear proliferation went beyond the control of the superpowers. America lost its first war, and our national spirit hit an all-time low.

They were years of social upheaval and violence. The winsome John F. Kennedy was assassinated by a warped social dropout. In shocking succession, his loss was followed by that of Martin Luther King, Jr., and Robert F. Kennedy. Civil rights became the focus of American attention while the nation confidently moved toward intervention in Vietnam, a little-known country halfway around the world. Riots and looting erupted in major cities, and then campuses became eerie battlegrounds. The nation struggled just to maintain peace at home while Vietnam's battles and body counts were telecast each night on the evening news. No one was prepared for what was happening.

The children of World War II were coming of age. The nation had not yet assessed or anticipated what they would be like. Our whole society had been restructured, and these children were its first product.

The early sixties had brought a new cultural phenomenon to America. The highways and crossroads of our nation were dotted with lonely faced, long-haired children with hand-painted, cardboard signs asking for a ride. California was best, but anywhere was better than where they were. Initially, with rare exception, they were harmless, benign social mutations.

Their tattered clothes, backpacks, and fragile sandals suggested their total abandonment of traditional values, behavior, and appearance. Their dress was characteristic, like a Brooks Brothers' suit or the blue uniform of a policeman. Their symbols were deeply rooted, proudly worn, and the badge of their individual commitment to a new life. It was a form of rebellion that touched almost a whole generation. Jerry Rubin, a leader of the political-activist movement during the sixties said, "My long hair had been as much a costume for me as suits and short hair for the middle class." [1]

It appeared as swiftly as a spring rain, but it gripped the nation like a long winter. These children believed they were free of cultural restraints and parental authority. They all had unique explanations for leaving home, but, to the careful listener, there was a certain sameness in their experiences.

Haight-Ashbury suddenly became more than an obscure Northern California community. It was both a symbol and a gathering place; a new mecca for the thousands of young people who were on the run.

Agonized parents were astonished to discover that law-enforcement officials could not return their runaway boys and girls. It was neither disinterest nor ineffective laws; it was the sheer avalanche of numbers that overwhelmed authorities. No one knows how many young people just disappeared. Estimates by experts range from two to six million each year for over a decade.

At first they were called *hippies*. It was a term of derision coined by the establishment. A new minority, they were despised by middle-class America, and their behavior and goals were not clear even to the children involved. They just wanted out. Out of home, away from limits, out of responsibility, and the freedom just to roam. These flower children and their V-shaped peace signs puzzled factory workers and executives alike. It seemed clear even at the beginning that their behavior was rebellion, but it appeared to have no focus, no direction, and no explanation. Dr. Nathan M. Pusey, president of Harvard University during the turbulent sixties, said,

"The youth of this generation are looking for a flag to wave, a creed to believe, and a song to sing." However, before the search for causes, there was the deep desire to separate themselves from what they believed was the modern social, political, and family trap. They rejected the status quo, but they had nothing better to offer society.

It was not, at the first, a structured movement. There were no recruiters, no study groups, no candidates; random thoughts, but no unified ideology and few identifiable leaders. That all came later when the storm erupted.

The establishment was outraged. Middle America was confused and stung. Despite their numbers, these wandering children, at least in the beginning, were not taken seriously. No reliable statistics were yet available, and the magnitude of the movement was not yet known. "It is a fad. It will just go away like crew cuts and white shoes," we were told. Hippie humor was fashionable and reflected some of the ignorance and mystery of the whole episode. The laughter would soon stop, however, and there would be a turn toward serious reflection.

Among informed sociologists, educators, and law-enforcement officials, a vivid sense that something new was happening began to surface. Not everyone took lightly what was emerging. Oh, there had always been runaways, but nothing like this. During this century there had been two prior waves of runaways. The depression of the thirties encouraged many to run just for survival. Hoboes wandered the highways looking for food and jobs. The forties transplanted thousands from their homeland in the Bible Belt to the wartime industrial centers of the Midwest. Their purpose, however, was clear. It had focus and direction from the outset. Irresistible economic and political forces were at work. The runaways of the sixties were totally different.

It is a simple-minded myth to believe there was a conspiracy among young people to leave home. There was no plan, no organization, but everywhere it was happening. These runaways did communicate with each other, but not through the traditional means used by modern America.

The movement was not geographical. In Minneapolis, Dayton, Indianapolis, and Peoria, parents were pleading for help in finding a thousand Phillips, Amys, and Andrews.

The movement cut across traditional class boundaries. Even the casual observer knew these children came from both rich and less affluent families. It was as near a classless society as America had ever seen. This only added to the general confusion.

The runaway movement was not economic rebellion. Although the prosperity of the sixties may have made mobility easier, it was not an effort to acquire more. They wanted no part of the corporate life-style or its financial advantages. They had no room for the keys to the executive washroom in the tiny cloth bags that contained all their possessions. Parents were stunned by children who cared little for summer homes, fashionable clothes, new automobiles, and lucrative careers.

The runaway movement had definable characteristics. These were the common denominators that parents and authorities observed in the lives of the individual children. Generally the characteristics were misunderstood, and the cause-and-effect relationship between life-style and philosophy became a matter of great debate. Marijuana was almost always found among these dropouts. The hard drugs and more dangerous hallucinogenics were introduced also, but they were more expensive and not as easily obtained. Sex outside of marriage was common, and disregard for conventional dress was the norm. They lived in unkempt apartment clusters or just slept at the beach or in parks. Thousands rarely spent two nights in the same place. Acid-rock music was universal in their subculture and general contempt for authority was a near certainty. The treatment they received at the hands of some frustrated law officials only heightened their social alienation.

It was universally believed that they were proudly immoral. It is true that they broke the Ten Commandments with complete abandonment, but a better word to describe their behavior and philosophy is amoral. There were few rules, and they demanded no standards from their peers. They were—as a class—totally devoid of a structured sense of right and wrong. It was as though they had been immunized against conscience.

The unconventional behavioral patterns were new and, therefore, understandably confusing to society. A cycle of mistrust and misunderstanding was begun. It was generally believed, at least by the unreflective, that the different habits and tastes in dress and music caused the alienation in society, of parent from child. No such causal relationship has ever been established. These characteristics no more produced rebellion than stripes produce a zebra. Stripes, at best, only identify zebras. The movement's life-style was a symptom of inward spiritual and emotional disorder. The causes were not so obvious. The root of the problem can be traced to the prewar years: it was social, philosophic, spiritual, and much more complex than generally believed. That is what this book is about.

It must be remembered that hundreds of thousands of these young people, like the prodigal son, returned home. A steady stream went back to relieved parents for over a decade. They found, however, that one "can never go back home." Everything was changed. Their experiences were now wider, and relationships were altered. Nevertheless, many were reunited with families and absorbed back into society. Often the telltale signs of life-style and dress betrayed their brief sojourn. Conflict in homes was common upon their return. Many found the economic price too high for their spirit of freedom and accepted the demands of the establishment for a "piece of the action." Some were disenchanted with their freedom. It carried far more responsibility than they had imagined. Another group is tragically gone forever. Many could not bear the despair of rejection and alienation by friends and family and took their own lives. Thousands of others died from unsterile needles or accidental drug overdoses. The casualty list is perhaps even greater than Vietnam. There was nothing noble in the sacrifice of these lives; no medals, no markers, and no national holidays. The nation wanted to forget, not to be reminded.

As with every movement, structure and ideology began to emerge out of aimlessness. Given time and opportunity, it was predictable that the vacuum of leadership, purpose, structure, and philosophy would be filled. As is frequently the case in new movements, the ideology develops after the fact, and the true believers readily accept it as an explanation for their behavior. Nonconformist behavior is an affront to society. Emotionally it needs a reason, a cause, an explanation. It does not have to be the correct reason. The youth of Hitler's Germany proved this. <u>Almost anything will satisfy those who are confused by their own actions.</u>

It must not be forgotten that these runaway children in the numbers we have discussed were incredible resources at the disposal of the "street smart." Millions of young people represent power—lots of it—if skillfully mobilized. There was money to be made. The Beatles, Elvis Presley, and then the more radical rock groups became multimillionaires quickly. Prostitution, drug pushing, and stealing were often the trades of innocent-looking children whose profits padded the pockets of their pimps. Those who had some morals soon developed spiritual callouses that seared the conscience.

The shrewd as well as the idealists saw readily available manpower for whatever particular cause they led. These children would march, carry signs, collect money, stuff envelopes, or anything else that messianic leaders needed done to advance their particular cause. The runaways ultimately became the cannon fodder and the fractured in the approaching, intense, social confrontations. They worked cheap, asked little in return, and were pliable; easy victims for exploitation. Not every leader was a conscious exploiter. Many leaders were victimized by their own rhetoric. They needed a cause as badly as their followers. They did not understand that their need was spiritual. Jerry Rubin, Eldridge Cleaver, Mark Rudd, and a hundred other such leaders have—with maturity—had dramatic changes in their philosophy and life-style. The same has occurred with many of their followers.

It would be a mistake to believe that this movement was exclusively an American cultural phenomenon. The same drama played all over Europe and Scandinavia. Although the news stories were in different languages, the parents wept the same tears. The thrust of this book, however, is primarily American, albeit the biblical and psychological principles apply universally.

These runaways were hurting and fractured emotionally. Uprooted, confused, and smoldering with rebellion, many were bright young people. It should be remembered that some of the nation's most intelligent young people walked the streets selling flowers and soliciting funds for esoteric causes.

The inevitable evolution came, and the children of the runaway movement started to cluster around ideas rather than life-styles. Three basic divisions emerged, and these youths began to gravitate toward one or more. The causes were social, political, and religious. Even the philosophies intermeshed. Young people had no difficulty participating in all of these pursuits. In each area the beginning was like a tiny rivulet, but it then became a mighty river of extremism at flood tide. Their crests came at different times, yet each movement's origin can be traced. It would indeed be comforting to know that the future is as easy to predict as history is to record. The worst, the most painful and dramatic, almost certainly lies in the future. Let's examine the structuring of the runaway movement.

Civil rights emerged first. The runaway Americans were drawn initially to the burning social issues of the early sixties. The Supreme Court had ruled in *Brown* v. *Board of Education of Topeka* in 1954 that segregation in public education denied equal protection of the laws. The civil-rights movement had come of age at precisely the right time to involve these young minds in need of a cause. Who could forget the March on Washington on August 28, 1963, when more than 200,000 Americans from all walks of life converged on the nation's capital. It constituted one of the largest single protests in American history. A very high percentage of the marchers who gathered at the Lincoln Memorial were young people. They mingled with congressmen and delegations from the establishment at the scene, and they could be heard lending their voices to "We Shall Overcome." Their unkempt clothes, unwashed long hair, and deep commitment identified them as the same kids at the side of the highways. It was the same crowd with a cause. Their empty hearts were ready when a young, black Baptist preacher shouted in typically Southern oratorical style, "I have a dream."

They fervently marched with Dr. Martin Luther King, Jr., into

Social
Political } movements
Religious

Selma, Memphis, and Montgomery. With arms locked they sat blocking traffic while red-necked policemen in utter frustration listened to their songs. They faced the police dogs, tear gas, and water hoses. They were arrested en masse in pursuit of their cause. Suffering with purpose was much easier than aimlessness with no meaning. It may have eased the pain to focus on a target. They spent nights in jails, superintended by frequently hostile guards. Some of their graves lie unmarked under the red clay of Alabama and Georgia and the black mud of Mississippi.

We do not mean to imply that King's cause of equal justice under the law was not noble, but rather that these children were ready for a cause. In fact, it was the very ideology of Martin Luther King, Jr., with his firm pacifism and doctrine of nonviolence, that restrained the growth of a more radical and violent civil-rights movement. Had the eventual key figure been militant like a Malcolm X, the whole story of the civil-rights movement and the activities of these young people would have been markedly different.

The riots came when King was assassinated in the late sixties, but they were not caused by the runaways. The riots were sparked by the young blacks who were without jobs and wanted into the establishment, not out. The army and National Guard were called out in Detroit, Watts, and Kansas City. Fortunately, King had cut his mark for pacifism deeply enough to avoid organized guerrilla warfare on a wide scale.

It is not true that all the people involved in the civil-rights movement were runaways. Andrew Young was well educated and, after a time in Congress, went on to become our United Nations Ambassador. Neither is it true that the civil-rights movement emerged because these young people were available. There was a real cause. It should be noted, however, that thousands of aimless wanderers gravitated to the cause. Their involvement helped the movement make a greater national impact and added momentum.

The antiwar and political activists emerged after the civil-rights struggle peaked. Vietnam was just a new cause. However, the leaders moved to the campus and attracted the more intellectual. Many of the young people who became a part of the antiwar protest had never officially run away from home. They had gone off to college, adjusted their life-styles and philosophies, but still maintained both economic and social contacts with home.

In 1965 Mario Savio led the free-speech movement at the Berkeley campus of the University of California. Jerry Rubin, one of the "Chicago Seven," got his start with Savio.

The civil-rights protestors wanted to reorganize the social system, while the campus radicals wanted to dismantle and redesign the political system.

Their movement reached a peak when President Lyndon B. Johnson announced he would not run for reelection.

The Students for Democratic Action with Mark Rudd at its helm, disrupted campus life all over America. Bombs exploded, administration buildings were barricaded, and students boycotted classes. There were mass demands for "rights," for participation in the design of policies and curricula, but without the experience to make alternate proposals.

Basically, students were looking for the limits of power—authority that could act. A student involved in the Kent State riots described a surging throng of students assaulting police cordons. Initially, the police fell back but quickly regrouped. The student assaults continued until the police strengthened their numbers with the National Guardsmen to halt the attack. The students then countered until they were overpowered by the authorities.The assault symbolized rebellious teens searching for a power larger and stronger than themselves.

The Jesus movement emerged last. It was a logical development. Belief in the occult and the supernatural had characterized these young people from the start. The frustration at failure to restructure the American political system was taking its toll. The vacuum of soul which precipitated the whole movement was still there. It was a simple step from the disappointments of civil-rights marches, drugs, and politics to the hope of peace held out by religious leaders.

It was, for some, an easy religion with little form, talking much about love, having little doctrinal content, and making few demands upon its converts. It was well fitted for their experience. These new believers had little time for conventional religion and almost totally rejected the institutional church. By now many of their personal lives were in shambles, and they were reaching out for anything to relieve their personal pain. So long as it did not resemble the impersonal religion of their parents, they were ready for help. The smell of pot was still clinging to their tattered clothes while bearded converts talked of "getting high on Jesus" at mass baptisms in the Pacific. This new religion was as confusing to parents as the values and life-style before their conversion.

The "Jesus freak" movement took on structure very quickly. Leaders emerged who devoted their ministries to the conversion of disillusioned hippies. The first Christian coffeehouse opened in 1967 in Haight-Ashbury. Centers were purchased and large organizations emerged. In the late sixties it was estimated that underground newspapers were distributed to as many as one million readers weekly. Drug-treatment programs were initiated. Courageous men like Arthur Blessitt left more traditional ministries to win these lonely converts. Many of these young people testified to being genuinely born again. Ironically, substantial funds to finance these ventures came out of the more affluent coffers of organized religion. The Jesus movement, for some, was a form of rebellion; for many, it brought salvation. Although it did rescue some of the radical, drug-crazed young people and lead them to a more conventional life-style, the movement also contained the elements of protest.

The Jesus people rejected the traditional church with its liturgy and formality. Emotions were unrestrained. Their meeting places avoided the symbols and architecture of the established church.

The theology of the parents, belief in Scripture, a sovereign God, a redemptive Christ, were all there; however, the outward expressions were all different. The Jesus people found themselves unwelcome in establishment churches, and their persistent talk of love was considered a sham and an affront by traditional worshippers.

It must also be said that the Jesus movement brought few young people back to their parents. Although they professed to know the same Christ as their parents, they were still far apart. It is interesting to note that the intensity of the Jesus movement lasted little longer than the firebrand supporters of the civil-rights movement or the antiwar protestors.

The Jesus movement, however, soon became the conservative wing of a dividing movement. Eastern mysticism found fertile soil and imported leaders like the Guru Maharaj Ji. They appealed to the more radical converts. Almost simultaneously, Sun Myung Moon and his brainwashed followers spread like a Middle Age contagion. Hare Krishna cultists with their shaved heads, their strange books, and their outstretched hands appeared at airports all over America. These radical religious groups controlled enormous sums of money and exercised an almost mystical hold on their novitiates.

There is no reason to believe we have seen the last of these new messiahs. Their names, causes, and leaders will be different; but so long as the root problem remains unsolved, new and more radical religious cults will continue to emerge.

The music of this entire movement was a unifying factor and a mode of expression. The songs had great appeal and were rallying points. Concerts brought people of similar life-styles together. Though music did not create the causes, it helped to communicate and provide mass expression. Adoring audiences vicariously experienced the intense emotions belted out in deafening decibels by costumed performers.

There were at least two types of music. Folk songs were typical of the King wing of the civil-rights movement. The plaintive strains of "We Shall Overcome" almost always could be heard. Joan Baez and Peter, Paul, and Mary added their ballads with a message. These ballads carried over into the war-protest movement. They were melodic and popular even among adults totally removed from political and social causes. The ballads were reminiscent of the folk music of black slaves of the 1880s. The music held out hope, but at the same time expressed deep despair and muted protest.

The other music was the hard rock of the Beatles and later acid-rock groups. Their songs expressed political and religious philosophy as well as obscenities and total rejection of the values of society. A majority of adults neither understood nor appreciated this musical expression. Jerry Rubin said, "I felt that 'yippie' was Beatles' music put to politics, and John Lennon was the most politically aware of the Beatles. In his Working Class Hero album John was singing to my soul." [2]

Woodstock and the hundreds of other concerts since the early sixties have brought rebels together. The crowds looked alike and the use of drugs was widespread. Law enforcement officials were—and are—almost helpless to control illegal activities of the crowds when 50,000 to 250,000 young people gather.

These young people are often alone in their own crowd. They come together with their peers, are protected by the crowd, but are still alone. In many cases it is a form of private personal release which some youths would compare to a religious experience. The acid rock is not sung by mass crowds, but by professional rock groups. The music has a mystical quality. Its message, form, language, and style overlapped. The romantic ballads of the civil-rights, antiwar, and Jesus movement all sounded alike. Some of the words were like a reminder of the evolutionary process of the whole movement. It began with aimlessness and drugs and climaxed with songs about "getting high on Jesus." Young people had grown accustomed to being high on drugs in the early sixties. Religion provided another high. Because lows uniformly followed the artificial "highs," there developed a frantic search for new "highs" that would last. Their whole existence moved toward self-centered, experience-oriented life.

Why did it all start? Something dramatic was happening. There is no precedent in all the history of mankind. In fact, Margaret Mead said, "This is the first generation in the history of man that needed books to teach him how to raise his young."

What are the causes of rebellion? What has happened to parents and their young? Parents are frightened and teenagers are distant. They live in the same house, eat at the same table, but hardly know each other. Sociologists are confused and give conflicting explanations and solutions. Child psychiatrists and psychologists often offer contradictory counsel. Dr. Benjamin Spock gave advice to a whole generation, and then admitted he was often misunderstood and sometimes wrong when he pontificated about child rearing.

Parents are so confused and fearful they are afraid to rely upon their own instincts. They have turned to the experts, and as an article in *Newsweek* magazine stated, "In the process [they] ended p relinquishing more responsibility." [3] Robert Coles, psychiatrist, observed, "We can't feed our children, discipline them, select schools, books, or games for them, even, it seems, have an ordinary conversation with them without consulting someone who claims to be in the know. This loss of self-respect and common sense is the principal reason why we turn to specialists, as if God had chosen to reveal Himself through them." [4]

Millions of young people, it should be remembered, have run away without ever leaving the four walls of their home. They drive the family car, eat at the family table, go to the neighborhood school, some even attend church, but they are thousands of miles away from their parents, emotionally and philosophically. An explanation needs to be provided for both groups—parents and children.

The factors are *not* simple, did *not* begin in the early sixties, and are *not* abating. The fact that the National Guard is gone from the campus of Kent State, that the mass looting of cities has stopped, that political conventions can be held without disruption, should not mislead us that the problems have gone away. Let us not forget that according to a spokesman for the National Association of Teachers over 60,000 teachers were assaulted in 1977 in the classroom. It is believed that the figure represents only a fraction of the attacks.

Although the nation's overall suicide rate has not measurably varied in the past half century, the rate for young people has nearly tripled between 1955 and 1975, from 4 suicides per 100,000 people to 11.8 per 100,000. The teen-suicide ratio is growing at an alarming rate. Suicides among young adults rose more than 100 percent between 1968 and 1976 according to government statistics.

The number of juveniles arrested for serious and violent crimes increased 1600 percent between the years 1952 and 1972, according to FBI figures. In the late seventies the rebellion is not restricted to teenagers. Drug addiction is reaching into elementary schools, and sexual experimentation is not uncommon among the preteen group. Recently, a number of kindergarten teachers in the Midwest noted a significant increase in defiant behavior among five-year-olds.

Rebellion is just taking a different form. The anger, the hate, the frustration are all still there. The young are now turning inward. In the sixties the largest undergraduate major was history. It should not be surprising to learn that in the seventies the largest undergraduate major is psychology. The parents of the seventies are also different. The pain of having their gifts rejected produced callouses. Some parents now say, "If I could do it over, I'd never have children." In a growing number of custody cases, neither the father nor the mother want the children. Understanding the causes will help some parents, will make others feel guilty, and hopefully will provide some solutions that can turn a nation around. The rest of this book is devoted to the reasons why it all happened and what both individual families and the nation must do if we are to avoid a more intense conflict or the numbness of despair.

Rebellious children have existed since the beginning of time. Cain rebelled against God and his parents, and murdered his brother. The sons of Jacob were jealous of their father's attention to their brother, Joseph, so, they sold him into slavery. The prodigal son left his father's house for a life of his own.

These stories, however, are examples we use. They are isolated incidents. Something new and dramatic has happened in our generation. Rebellion against the life-style, values, and beliefs of parents has become a national epidemic. Like the Bubonic Plague in Europe, it has touched almost every family in some way.

Why now? What happened to America? It's almost as though a new and deadly bacteria had been released that singled out teenagers, modifying their behavior. Ministers, social scientists, and child psychiatrists are frantically scurrying around digging for solutions. Answers to individual cases are offered, but we need some broader answers that explain why a whole generation of young people went wrong. For five thousand years, the behavior of children was predictable. Suddenly, all that changes. There must be some common answers to a most common problem.

Chapter 2

Children and the Reshaping of America

The year was 1929. Herbert Hoover had won a stunning victory over Al Smith in the last presidential election. Only a year before, in his last preelection campaign speech, he had appraised the state of the American economy in a major address: "We are nearer today to the ideal of the abolition of poverty and fear from the lives of men and women than ever before in any land."

A sense of economic euphoria gripped the nation as bootblacks, beauticians, and bankers all had hot tips on exploding stocks. Affluence was eternal, it was believed, and was now the American way. Suddenly, it all ended on October 29, 1929. The stock market had fallen 50 percent in four days. All the optimism and support by the directors of major New York banks did not help, and promises that the market would quickly rebound were without foundation. It is estimated that the paper losses were 30 billion dollars as a result of the crash, an amount larger than the national debt at that time.

The bubble had burst. Almost overnight wild speculation, affluence, and confidence turned into a nightmare of breadlines and joblessness. Two years later, the night before Roosevelt's inauguration, there were restrictions placed on banks in all forty-eight states, but

41

already 5,737 banks had failed. In 1931 over 32,000 businesses went bankrupt. In 1930 there were 6 million people out of work and when unemployment bottomed out in 1932, there were 12 million Americans without jobs.

The mood of the country changed to grim despair. One man recalls that as a child of seven, he walked the streets on early Sunday mornings in search of the rare coins that may have been dropped on Saturday nights. Families were drawn together by the desperation of those times. They needed each other.

The nation struggled for a decade toward economic recovery. A climate was being created, however, that would make vocational transitions a necessity. Later events would combine with this economic catastrophe to produce a strain on the traditional role of the family in modern America.

✳ *It was December 7, 1941.* Only two hours before, the sun had risen, lighting the sparkling blue waters of Hawaii. At 7:55 A.M. a strike force of 360 airplanes began a methodical attack on Pearl Harbor. Japanese fighter planes and thundering bombers came in waves. With total surprise and little resistance, they attacked the 94 American ships trapped in the harbor. At 8:25 A.M. a second attack of dive bombers and torpedoes was launched. By 10:00 A.M. on that Sunday the battle was over.

The carnage was incredible. The Japanese had accomplished most of their goals. All eight of the American battleships were damaged so badly they could not be used. Three of seven cruisers were sunk, and three destroyers were wrecked. The battleship *Oklahoma* had capsized, and the battleship *Arizona* was blown up, leaving eleven hundred of its crew in a watery grave. Over two thousand men were killed and another two thousand wounded.

The sneak attack had destroyed a significant part of the United States Pacific Naval Fleet. America was at war. On December 8, at the request of President Franklin Delano Roosevelt, Congress declared war on Japan, and on December 11 on Germany and Italy. The whole nation was touched in some way. Over thirteen million men were inducted into the armed forces before the conflict ended.

The country had to be reorganized overnight to win the war. Again, the family in America experienced the pressure of dramatic change.

＊*It was July 20, 1969.* The eerie figure of Neal A. Armstrong appeared on television screens all over the world as he set foot on the surface of the moon. It had begun on Wednesday, July 16, when a 360-foot *Saturn V* rocket blasted off from the John F. Kennedy Space Center on the eleventh mission of Project Apollo. After establishing an orbit around the moon, Armstrong and two other astronauts, Edwin E. Aldrin, Jr., and Michael Collins, prepared to disengage the landing craft from the mother ship. The smaller craft settled onto the moon's surface just as planned.

Armstrong and Aldrin walked with a strange waddle in near weightlessness as they cautiously explored the area about their ship. They planted a flag, collected rock samples, carried out experiments, and then walked back up the steps into the moon craft. The service-module's rocket thrust them back into a moon orbit and an eventual rendezvous with the mother spacecraft, as Collins awaited their return. Safely back to earth, out of the water, and onto the U.S.S. *Hornet* they came. The President was aboard the ship to welcome them, and it is estimated that over one billion people viewed their return as electronic space satellites beamed their signals around the world.

It is incredible by contrast that in 1932, only thirty-seven years earlier, the attention of the whole world was on Amelia Earhart, the first woman to fly solo from North America to Europe. The nation turned its attention from crossing an ocean to rocketing through space; a quantum leap in technology had been made. The technological revolution that brought space travel reordered our lives, and, in one generation, the whole civilized world had changed. The Industrial Revolution with its new source of energy, the combustion engine, came to America in the late nineteenth century. A swift succession of improvements and inventions climaxed in the second half of the twentieth century with the technological revolution, spawned by the miracle of electronics and the computer. More scientists were alive at one time than had lived in all previous generations of mankind, and the volume of knowledge was doubling every seven years.

Three major events occurred in one half a century that reshaped our social and political structure as a nation: an economic reorganization, a global war, and a technological revolution. The stock market crash in 1929, the attack on Pearl Harbor in 1941, and the moon walk in 1969 symbolize powerful events that challenged American family life. Major population shifts, new work and family roles, changing educational demands, leisure time, and easy mobility snowballed in their effects on our country and on us as individuals.

Apparent cause-and-effect relationships may be deceptive. Social change does not necessarily cause teenagers to rebel against the values and theology of their parents. Technology and industrialization are not inherently bad. We cannot, however, ignore the enormous pressures of these years.

It was in the wake of World War II that many young people began to rebel. A new expression came into common usage, *juvenile delinquency*. Special judicial courts were set up to judge their "crimes" and to protect their welfare and that of their families. The significant increase in mental-hospital admissions of young people tells another part of the story. We have made of the misbehaviors of children either a crime to be judged or a sickness to be treated. Neither is appreciably turning the tide. If we are to do that, we must teach parents how to be parents, and we must reparent the confused children.

Let us trace the events of the last generation and their impact on the family.

The Nation Is Reshaped in One Generation

AMERICA LEAVES THE FARM. In the eighteenth and nineteenth centuries, farming was the most important American occupation. Farmers were isolated, independent, and largely self-sufficient. The single-family farm, although never the utopia it was made out to be, was a part of the great American dream. But things down on the farm began to change, and to change quickly.

The machine was rapidly revolutionizing man's life and work

machinery
electricity
chemical

habits. Productivity was increased with new technology. In the 1920s, a massive mechanization program began on the farm. Very soon horses and mules disappeared as a primary source of power. In less than forty years the cotton sack, the hoe, and the small single-family farm would be relics of the past. A substantial portion of the nation's agribusiness is now managed by corporate executives with access to computers and space satellites to forecast crops.

A major contribution to the leap in farm production was the widespread introduction of electricity. Electric power brought light to farm buildings, milking machines to dairies, electric fences to ranches, refrigeration, the telephone, the radio, and, finally, the television to farm families. The laboratory brought new chemical compounds that improved production and controlled noxious weeds.

The natural impact on farm life can be clearly illustrated by the statistics themselves. In 1820 one farmer produced enough food for himself and three others. By 1960 he fed himself and thirty others. It was all very simple; new machinery, electricity, and a chemical revolution made it possible for one man to farm more land. *1975- 57 people*

These improvements did not necessarily mean that everything on the farm was developing as planned and that everyone was enjoying prosperity. Although technology was increasing productivity, the American farmer, in the very midst of these rapid changes, suffered unbearable poverty during the twenties and thirties. The farmer never regained the purchasing power he had before World War I. The farmers' distress in the twenties turned to despair in the thirties. The Great Depression had a more disastrous effect on the farmer than his urban counterpart. Historian Arthur M. Schlesinger, Jr., said, "No group in the population, except perhaps the Negro workers, was more badly hit by the depression . . . farm prices had fallen more than fifty percent." [1]

The truth is that a number of factors all converged that produced a mass exodus from the farm. Because of improved methods, fewer farmers were needed, and those who stayed found their lives different from their fathers. Technology forced young farmers who remained on the farm to the university as agribusiness became a science. The rural-depression hardship caused the majority of young people to be unhappy with the farms. Electric power along with radio, the telephone, the automobile, and finally television, ended the isolation of the farmer, and World War II provided a route of escape. Over 3 million boys from rural America were drafted into the armed forces during the forties. While some farmers became soldiers, others were attracted to the war industries. Neither group ever returned to the farm in significant numbers.

Dramatic change came, and America moved to town almost overnight. In 1870, sixty of every one hundred Americans worked in agriculture, but by 1960 only six of every one hundred had farm-related jobs. Single-family farms grow fewer in number each year, and only eighty thousand new farmers are needed annually. A majority of those jobs are filled by family members. The shift to urban life was a natural part of the economic, social, and technological revolution. Those living on the American farm dropped from 24.9 percent of the population in 1930 to 4.8 percent in 1970, according to statistics compiled by the U.S. Census Bureau.

2. **THE YOUNG MEN MOVE TO THE FACTORIES.**   While disenchantment grew on the farm during the poverty of the depression, the small-family businesses in the city were facing some of the same pressures. World War II produced huge factories, and new technology improved assembly-line production and automation. The small family business had difficulty competing and became less attractive and less profitable. More and more young men from the farms and the cities took jobs in industry. For the first time in the forties, America became a nation of factory and office workers. It was not only an economic reorganization; it brought a most significant change of life-style.

3. **THE WOMEN GO TO WORK.**   World War II brought women into the factory by the hundreds of thousands. It was considered an act of patriotism for women to assist in a time of national emergency. While millions of young men fought World War II, women helped make the instruments of war.

When the war ended, women began to retreat from the work force for a period of time. However, a new women's work movement began in the fifties and has grown steadily ever since. In 1870 only 15 out of one hundred workers in America's labor force were women or girls. The Labor Department reported that in October, 1978 of the total civilian labor force of 101,555,000 nearly 45 percent were women.

The role of the woman as well as the number of women in modern industry has changed significantly. Woman is no longer just an extension of man. Traditionally, women did clerical work or menial tasks in factories. That is now untrue. Women in large numbers work alongside men in assembly plants at equal wages. They have begun to appear in the corporate boardrooms and now routinely travel, unaccompanied, from city to city doing the work that once was exclusively reserved for men.

The women's movement of the past twenty years has grown in its power. While women continued to work, their pay and benefits were often less advantageous than men's. An indignant, fighting spirit among women was fanned into a blaze of anger. We have seen the gentleness of a woman's real strength changed to a rigid fanaticism at some points.

THE CHILDREN GET A BABY-SITTER. As women moved into the job market, provision had to be made for preschool children. Professionally operated private day-care centers during World War II were virtually unknown.

Even today, as day-care centers are more readily available, 60 percent of working mothers arrange to have a relative care for their children, mostly in homes. Only 10 percent of working mothers use center-based care. However, that percentage has doubled since 1965.

The day-care-center movement is currently developing into big business. Its growth is very significant. It is all now neatly organized, franchised, computerized. Children are appropriately provided for while mom works.

Although materialism may prompt some of those in the booming market of preschools and day care for children, many of them are truly concerned with the welfare of children. While college aptitude scores are dropping and young people are quitting school in large numbers, many people are looking for reasons. Even early-school children are failing, and it has been hoped that preschools might help prevent the losing habit. For some, it may work. There is concern, however, that parents could feel so sure of the excellence of these centers, that they would increasingly abdicate their own responsibility. There is no substitute for the love, care, and enjoyment of a child by his own parents.

With all its input, positive or negative, there is no doubt that the increasing popularity of early-childhood schooling is taking children away from the home and family. It is too soon to evaluate the effects of this on the developing child.

⑤ **MOTHERS GET SOME HELP.** The work of the woman in the 1930s was drudgery and required up to sixteen hours each day. Much of the water came from wells, laundry was boiled with home-made soap, and each dish was washed by hand. Clothes were made by mothers who occasionally splurged by ordering from a Sears' catalog. Reliable birth control was not available, and increasing numbers of children often added burdens rather than joy.

Work in the home, however, has now followed the same pattern as in industry. Electric dishwashers, sophisticated ovens, and ranges with computerlike dials are standard equipment in new homes. Electric washers and dryers, can openers, mixers, blenders, knives, egg poachers, garbage disposals, vacuum cleaners, crock pots, food processors, frost-free refrigerators, trash compactors are all common in middle-class homes. The new technology has made labor-saving devices affordable and the gadgetry infinite and imaginative. It now borders on the absurd.

Precooked and pre-prepared foods abound. Biscuits come out of cans, potatoes are precut and often precooked, pies and casseroles are frozen. Mothers can buy frozen lasagna, charcoal-broiled steak, or orange juice. Meals require a fraction of the time to prepare compared to what they did twenty years ago. Just in case mom is too tired to pop frozen food in the microwave, a score of fast-food chains are just around the corner.

Wash-and-wear fabrics have reduced the time mom once spent at the ironing board. At the same time diaper services and disposable diapers have eliminated many hours from the care of the very young. Cleaning services now care for a substantial portion of the clothes of blue-collar workers as well as the dress shirts of executives.

Minicomputers are now being marketed for home use that will further reduce the workload and responsibility in the home. Retailers now promise that mass production will place them in the reach of most homes very soon.

The average woman, with all the new labor-saving devices, can do her entire work at home in no more than 25 percent of the time required of her mother. This is one of the major factors that has allowed her to move into the job market.

6. THE AMERICAN AUTOMOBILE. The American automobile has become the symbol of economic prosperity. It is axiomatic that record automobile sales mean good times for everybody. The housing industry flourishes, and retail sales rise proportionately. It is the new American Way.

Drive by any high school in America and you will see that large areas for student parking are as essential as the gymnasium. The child who has no access to "wheels" is socially deprived.

Mothers who work also find it either necessary or convenient to have an automobile. It is not uncommon in urban America, then, for the family to have three vehicles. Over 10 million American families own 3 or more cars. In 1976 there were 110,351,327 automobiles registered in America.

7. THE GOVERNMENT GETS INVOLVED. Before the depression, the American people were characterized by rugged individualism. The depression drove America to government for economic solutions, and World War II, the single greatest national emergency in our history, necessitated giving the federal bureaucracy unprecedented power. The nation has become progressively more reliant upon Washington with each passing year. Over 35 percent of all money spent in the economy is spent by local, state, and federal government. A startling fifteen million people, or one of each six people employed, works for city, state, or federal government.

A confusing welter of overlapping welfare programs provides government assistance to an incredible number of persons. When one combines the people receiving assistance from Aid to Families with Dependent Children, the General Assistance Program, the Food Stamp Program, the Supplemental Security Program, and the Housing for the Elderly Program, more than twenty-five million people receive some form of welfare assistance. Parallel with the rise of government bureaucracies was the abdication of responsibility by the extended family for their own members.

The government makes it possible for millions of women to live without husbands and take care of children. Social Security has greatly relieved the responsibility children feel toward parents in advancing years. The wedge between parents and children begins in preschool and continues now to the grave.

 THE FAMILY GETS A TELEVISION. Television has come to virtually every home in America as a result of electronic advances and the new technology. Almost every child is exposed to its influence. According to a television survey by A. C. Nielsen, "Children under five watch an average of 23.5 hours of TV a week. Today's typical high-school graduate has logged at least 15,000 hours before the screen—more time than he has spent on any other activity except sleep. At present levels of advertising and mayhem, he will have been exposed to 350,000 commercials and vicariously participated in 18,000 killings. The conclusion is inescapable: after parents, television has become perhaps the most potent influence on beliefs, attitudes, values, and behaviour of the young." [2]

The Traditional Family Structure Is Threatened

Incredible pressure was imposed on the traditional family relationships by the reshaping of America. It is wishful thinking, however, to somehow believe that we can return to the quiet, rural life before 1930. It is important, however, that we clearly understand what has happened so that our response can be reasoned.

The change in the American family structure that occurred between 1930 and 1960 was profound. It has had a devastating effect upon children. Traditional roles and relationships that were believed natural and inviolate began changing very rapidly. The effects of those changes were not observed carefully enough while they were occurring. We need to understand, analyze, and compensate for them. Adjustments can and must be made to meet the crisis of social pressure on the American home. Let's trace the developments in the home and the consequent effect upon children.

THE HOME IS FRAGMENTED AND REDESIGNED. The home was first fragmented vocationally when the man's work separated him from his family. Away from the farm and the small family business, an individual became an economic unit rather than part of a family.

During the years that America was principally a rural country, the man of the house worked long, hard hours in the fields, but earning a living was, of necessity, a family affair. We must remember that the wife worked, but it was unpaid family work and her labor was closely associated with her husband's.

The whole family arose before daybreak, and each family member was assigned a job to do. The father and sons started the fire in the winter, milked the cows, and fed the stock. At the same time, the wife and daughters were preparing breakfast and jointly doing the work in the home. Frequently, hired hands ate meals with the family as a part of their wages.

The children were taken out of school during spring planting and fall harvest. It was not so much puritan ethic or self-discipline, it was a matter of survival. The entire family had to labor or starve. When families lived on the farm, children worked alongside their fathers. Both the wife and children understood his labor. When small family businesses were operated in the cities, they were also a part of the children's life. It was considered normal for a son to assist, then follow his father in his vocation. Children were an economic asset. In modern America, they are considered by some to be a financial liability and an inconvenience.

Factory and office work changed those relationships. Fathers now left for work before daybreak to work inside huge and mysterious bleak buildings. When they returned at night, darkness was usually falling. Their work was alien, distant, unknown, as the dark side of the moon.

Charles A. Reich described life before the changes came: "Most people were born, lived, worked, and died in the same place, among people they knew and saw every day. There was no separation between work and living. Ties to the community were strong and seldom severed; each man lived within a circle which did not depend upon his own action, began before him, and lasted beyond him. Food and shelter were communal enterprises; no one grew fat or starved alone. The scale of everything was small: tools, houses, land, villages. There were no large, impersonal institutions— apartment houses, factories, or hospitals." [3]

The technological revolution of the last half of this century only heightened the sense of impersonalization and alienation. All that is changed, and it is ever so clear when discussing it with today's youth. When interviewing children about their father's vocation, over 90 percent said they had no part whatsoever in the father's job. A large percentage did not fully understand what function their father played in industry. The new work patterns brought cleavages to families. Reich said it well: "The village community was broken as men were forced to seek jobs in factories or cities. Family ties shattered for the same reason. The apartment replaced the village and the family home." [4]

The family separation is not exclusively a problem of factory workers in this new world. Fathers with executive positions in modern corporations were facing other job pressures that estranged them from their wives and children. Large numbers of fathers were given jobs that required regular travel. Children often do not see their fathers from Monday morning until Friday night. The mother is left with the principal task of discipline, character building, and managing the daily affairs of the family. The positive influence of a father is sacrificed for job opportunity and advancement. Then, it is more than travel. The long hours at the office leave little opportunity for parent-child interaction.

The vocational cleavage of the home was heightened when mothers went to work. Working mothers first reflected the new values of America. The family had its fill of poverty in the Depression. In reaction both mother and father would work in order to have all the nice things they missed during youth. When the wife from the late forties onward took a job outside the home, the purpose was generally different from previous decades. She worked to supplement the family income, not for survival. She worked for a higher standard of living that brought a second car, a new home, or electronic gadgetry. The children would be given things rather than mother's presence.

Although she began to work initially to supplement family income, families soon found themselves economically hooked. Thirty-year home mortgages and two automobiles were long-term financial commitments. Now it became clear that the woman's paycheck was essential as the family permanently adjusted its living standard upward.

If the family structure was weakened by dads leaving home for job opportunities, it was crucially fractured as mothers went to work. It was not, however, the fact of the mother's working that created the problem. Generally it was the reason for her leaving the home that made it a problem or not. If mothers worked out of personal or financial necessity, most children could understand and even appreciate her efforts. As they realized her working relieved financial burdens and offered extra benefits to the family, they could tolerate her absence and even help about the house to support her.

Children are extremely sensitive, however, and if they sensed that mom had gone to work to escape the burden of their presence or to avoid a strained marriage to their dad, they were threatened. If she felt guilt, as many working mothers do, she would often try to alleviate that by giving money, privileges, or things to the children. Often working mothers out of the same guilt feeling, or simply fatigue, fail to discipline their children and even rescue them from the healthy disciplines of reality. This is the sort of family fracture that can totally destroy a home.

When women moved into the job market in large numbers, it was also reflected in their attitudes toward marriage in general and their husbands in particular. In effect, their liberation began.

The wife found a new sense of independence and self-worth apart from her husband. Her job, like her husband's, became important to her beyond the economic benefits. A sense of achievement, new friends, mobility, and a new freedom all came as a natural part of work.

Women in general became aware of the contribution they made to industry and soon discovered that they generally received lower pay for the same work. Discrimination against women in industry is an undeniable fact. The pressure for the ratification of the Equal Rights Amendment is a natural part of this evolution. It is questionable that its passage will benefit the American family.

The man had used his mobility for years to engage in extramarital affairs. It was now the woman's turn. While no reliable statistics are yet available, the experts agree that the increase in the number of working women has had a direct relational effect on the increase in extramarital affairs. Sexual values began to change, and divorce rates have grown alarmingly.

Women who work are less likely to be submissive to their husbands. In a great measure, the woman's economic dependence upon the male has steadily decreased since the fifties, and women, in general, are exercising more freedom. Their options in life have been increased infinitely.

Men whose wives work find it essential to help prepare meals, go to the Laundromat, diaper babies, and, in general, do chores once thought exclusively reserved for women. Both husband and wife have less time to spend with children after work hours. It is important to note that the divorce rate rose in direct proportion to the rise of married women in the work force. In 1940 little more than 20 percent of married women worked. However, by 1978, 48 percent of all married women were a part of the labor force.

By 1975, one in every two marriages failed. The divorce rate had doubled between 1963 and 1975, and today, in the United States it is the highest in the world. The ratio of divorce to marriages increased from one to six in 1940 compared with one to two in 1975. During that same period of time, the percentage of women in the work force doubled.

A majority of American housewives who do not work are bored when their children start to school. In upper income levels, a wife may hire a cleaning woman one day a week which will enable her to volunteer her services at the local hospital. The fact that a woman does not work outside the home does not guarantee that she will be more devoted to her children.

A whole generation of children is being raised with minimal personal touch with mother. The influence of the day-care center is not yet fully known, but some preliminary observations are being made. The results are not encouraging. Children raised in day-care centers, while working better with other children, are having considerable difficulty doing activities by themselves. The discipline and training for the development of individual identity and integrity simply are not present. James Dobson wrote, "The Russian government is currently abandoning its child care network because they have observed the . . . inescapable fact: employees of the state simply cannot replace the one-to-one influence of a mother with her own child." [5]

It is common for the teenager to work in modern America. However, in urban areas his work is rarely associated with his father's vocation. Often as the father is arriving home from work, the teenager, having finished his day at school, is leaving for a part-time job at McDonald's. Even family meals, which once were traditionally shared, are often eaten in shifts.

The work patterns have created different environments, as well as eliminating the possibility for children to spend time with the father.

Often the father is in bed when the teenager finishes work. Fathers and children live in different worlds where neither has shared the other's experiences.

The student car normally means a part-time job to pay the monthly bank payments, fuel, and rising insurance cost. These young people are learning sound principles of responsibility, but it also means mobility. It is another tool to carry teens far away from home. A car virtually insures that a teenager will spend less time with his parents and more with his friends. The student with a car invariably assists his less fortunate friends to explore the city while mom and dad work.

The car has given teens time and opportunity to engage in activities that are harmful. Peer pressure is probably at its peak in an automobile filled with six teens.

Now the cycle is complete. Daddy is at the factory, mother is at the office, the little ones are in day-care centers, and teenagers are at part-time jobs. Occasionally, on the weekend, they coincidentally meet for a meal and listen to lectures about "why we can't communicate anymore."

The fragmentation and redesign of the home was an evolutionary process and it most certainly goes beyond its four walls. In the thirties, the clan-type family was typical. A mother and father cared for their children with grandparents, uncles, and aunts nearby. Fifty years ago half the families in the United States included at least one extra adult; today, fewer than 5 percent do.

Mobility in the fifties and sixties brought the nuclear family—a mother and father with their children living several hundred miles from relatives. Now, even the nuclear family is fading. Fifty-one percent of American mothers with school-age children are working outside the home, two thirds of them at full-time jobs. All indications are that the traditional "nuclear family," with the husband working and the wife raising children and taking care of household chores, is dying. Only 14 percent of the population now fits into that category.

High divorce rates of the late sixties and seventies have produced the single-parent family. Over eleven million children now live in single-parent homes. Since 1960 the number of such families has grown seven times as fast as the two-parent families.

Changing values now allow children to be raised in family situations that were totally foreign to America even twenty-five years ago. Cohabitation without marriage is a growing cultural phenomenon. In 1977 there were 1,506,000 such relationships.

FAMILY OF THE FUTURE.   Mothers are bearing children through artificial insemination. James Hefley wrote in an article that each year there are 20,000 births as a result of artificial insemination and that an estimated 200,000 living babies are believed to have been conceived through this process. He further speculates, ". . . a woman who desires to conceive but not gestate her own baby may have her fertilized embryo transplanted to the womb of a host mother who will, for a fee, carry it to maturity." [6]

A growing number of adults living in homosexual relationships are rearing children. Although the census bureau does not currently maintain these statistics, there is other evidence of the growing social change. In an article for *The Star*, published in New York, Steve Dunleavy reported that at a meeting of lesbians in the summer of 1978 on the campus of Illinois State University in Normal, Illinois, a resolution was adopted calling for 500,000 test-tube babies within four years to be raised, using sperm donated from practicing homosexuals. The goal is to rear 200,000 in New York City to help build a political power base for a new social order.

The cultural and familial changes of the past four decades have occurred with lightning rapidity and profound consequences. The results of recent value changes and medical discoveries may produce a new type of family shock.

THE HOME IS INVADED.   The home was once a refuge from bad influences. Television, however, has invaded virtually every home from the exclusive penthouses of Manhattan to the shanties of coal-mining towns in West Virginia.

The new technology has made it possible for the very young child, with a flip of the dial, to bring violence, sex, obscenity, as well as an assault upon traditional values and roles into the home.

Television, like it or not, has become the most powerful teaching tool in America. It is a far more powerful influence than the public-school system and in most cases the church.

Television, with all of its visual magic, implants ideas with greater force than the schools. Television is, of course, a morally neutral tool. It can be used for good or bad. However, it seems clear that those who control programming in television have rejected the traditional values of America. Adultery, single-parent homes, violence, homosexuality, divorce, remarriage, and defiance of parents are portrayed as the social norm.

The child slowly accepts what is portrayed as normal or glamorized as a guide for his behavior. The parent sits silently in the same room while an electronic outsider invades his home attacking everything the parent believes. The child is told alcohol and cigarettes will make one chic and glamorous, extramarital sex is normal, parents are stupid, and father is a bigot.

The televison is rarely controlled, and parents relinquish their responsibility to teach to an electronic alien. Subtly, both communication and shared values are destroyed by what Kenneth Keniston, chairman of the Carnegie Council on Children called "this flickering blue parent occupying more of the waking hours of American children than any other single influence." [7] The television is often used as a substitute for the day-care center. Clearly, a great part of television programming helps to fragment family life rather than strengthen it. The productions of Norman Lear are not a reflection of what America is, but what those who share his values want it to be. His productions represent the ultimate in television as a teaching tool.

Materialism invaded the home. Advertising with its powerful means of modern design, the radio, the TV, and sophisticated psychological studies has learned how to create a craving for things. The affluence of modern America has provided the wherewithal to acquire while social developments have made families vulnerable targets.

Parents who grew up in the Depression find it difficult to resist the urge to give their children those things they did not have. Guilt in parents who neglect their children in favor of deeper commitments to careers try to compensate for absences with things. Finally, the impersonal society with its loss of close family relationships has tempted people to try material things in an effort to satisfy the need for a sense of acceptance and community.

Much of the despair of the young, as well as their rejection of the life-style of their parents, has come from the realization that things do not satisfy. Materialism, as a way of life, is a disruptive influence in America's homes. Things can never replace relationships.

THE CHILDREN ARE NEGLECTED. Busy parents scurry from job to other responsibilities. Mother and father work while teenagers seek part-time jobs after school. The TV, the school, the day-care center, the church have all become substitute parents.

Children are not close enough to learn by observing and listening what adult life is like. Sociologist Sarane Boocock of the Russell Sage Foundation reports that some mothers devote as little as fifteen minutes a day to actual communication with their preschoolers.

She also reported that based on interviews and surveys, "Very few children eat dinner regularly with their parents . . . and few spend as much as two hours a day with adults other than teachers." W

Newsweek claims, "Nearly two million school age children are not enrolled in schools. Another million are 'latchkey' children who come home to an empty house . . . and spend most of their time with their peers." [9]

The fathers, caught up in America's quest for vocational advancement, are also spending less and less time with children. Dr. Urie Bronfenbrenner reported that a group of researchers discovered some astounding things in a study of middle-class fathers. Microphones were attached to the shirts of small children to learn the actual contact with their fathers. The average amount of time spent by these fathers with their children was 37 seconds per day. The direct encounters averaged only 2.7 minutes daily. [10]

The Believer's Response to the Crisis of the Children

In the past half-century, America has experienced the most profound social revolution in the recorded history of mankind. It happened with great speed, and much of what it wrought cannot be
undone. There is nothing in the economic, social, and technological
history of man with which we can compare it. The last generation is
unique, without parallel.

Alvin Toffler, the futurologist, reflects upon the significance and
speed with which change has come to our world: "For we have not
merely extended the scope and scale of change, we have radically
altered its pace. We have in our time released a totally new social
force—a stream of change so accelerated that it influences our sense
of time, revolutionizes the tempo of daily life, and affects the very
way we 'feel' the world around us. We no longer 'feel' life as men
did in the past. And this is the ultimate difference, the distinction
that separates the truly contemporary man from all others. For this
acceleration lies behind the impermanence—the transience—that
penetrates and tinctures our consciousness, radically affecting the
way we relate to other people, to things, to the entire universe of
ideas, art and values. . . . When we speak of the rate of change, we
refer to the number of events crowded into an arbitrarily fixed inter-
val of time. . . ." He also stated, "Indeed, a growing body of reputable opinion asserts that the present movement represents nothing
less than the second great divide in human history, comparable in
magnitude only with that first great break in historic continuity, the
shift from barbarism to civilization." [11]

The new social structure has provided fertile soil for child rebellion and family disunity. The story of the reshaping of the American
family suggests the relationship between social pressures and the
disintegration of the home. The statistical relationship is too obvious
to ignore. But is it theologically accurate to argue that social pressures or environment causes teenagers to rebel and parents to neglect the commands of God? Does poverty, technology, industrialization, or mobility cause children to rebel?

Those who take the Bible seriously have always maintained that man is not the product of his environment, but, rather, he is a sinner because he is a part of Adam's fallen race. Adam sinned, and, because we are a part of Adam's race, we are sinners. The Bible describes man as spiritually dead and thoroughly degenerate.

Those who look to the Bible for authority have maintained that cleaning up the ghettos, providing better education and better housing would not change a man's heart. It is theologically inaccurate to suggest that social change produces sin. How can we reconcile the apparently bad influences of social history and the Bible statement about man's sinful nature?

The paradox is simply explained and is not a contradiction of Bible truth or principle. We are not the product of our environment, but we do reflect the spiritual quality of our environment.

It is also true that the influence of culture that has tended to invade the sanctity of the home in the last generation can be resisted. It is not inevitable that living in the pressure of an evil environment must destroy the morals of children and alienate them from their parents. It is avoidable, and there are clear examples to demonstrate it. We are not the helpless victims of our environment.

American families, while perhaps not able to trace social history over the past forty years, are keenly aware that something is wrong. A search even by the humanists is currently underway to find the way out. In the process, a number of options have been tried. Some are totally unsuccessful, and others only moderately successful in resisting the detrimental effects of society. But, there is an answer. Let's examine the efforts at neutralizing the bad effects of social pressure on children.

TRIAL AND ERROR. A number of ideas are now being tried in an effort to cope with social pressure on children. Only modest success has been achieved. The glaring error has been the neglect of the authority of the Bible. The best textbook on child rearing is a complete copy of both Old and New Testaments. Any method, technique, or philosophy that ignores the Bible is incomplete at best and inaccurate at worst. In the frantic search for solutions by pained parents, some serious errors have been made.

PARENT EFFECTIVENESS TRAINING.   Dr. Thomas Gordon and a host
of associates have introduced a technique for rearing modern children which its proponents guarantee to succeed. Dr. Gordon's basic
thesis might be called "accommodation." He argues that because
young people of the twentieth century have been reared in a social
climate that emphasizes rights rather than responsibilities, we
should adjust our methods to the new values of children.

Dr. Gordon suggests, "Today's youth are discharging their
parents—informing them that their services are no longer needed.
. . . The lesson for parents is that they can be helpful consultants to
their children—they can share their ideas, experiences, wisdom—if
they remember to act like an effective consultant so they do not get
fired by the clients whom they wish to help." [12]

Dr. Gordon stresses what he calls "logical consequences" and
insists that children be involved in making their standards. He
suggests forming a family council and that children be allowed to
vote on whatever limits are established. He justifies the parental
manipulation of these council meetings as a necessary evil to obtain
the desired results. The whole concept ignores absolute truth and
the responsibility of parents to establish norms. [13]

THE CHRISTIAN SCHOOL.   Hundreds of thousands of parents have
turned to the Christian school to protect children from deteriorating
social values and behavior. Although it is true that some schools
were born in an effort to avoid integration and busing, many others
clearly wanted to protect their children from schools whose invasive
influence and values violated the principles practiced in the home.
Although Catholic and Jewish schools are quite old, only in the last
twenty years has there been a significant increase in the number of
conservative Christian schools. Quality Christian education, in
evangelical circles, has the potential to become a significantly positive force to support the Christian home.

Theoretically, the Christian school movement should minimize
the bad social pressure on the home. A child, it is argued, during the
formative years is under the influence of godly teachers and among

saintly peers as he learns reading, writing, and arithmetic. The movement, however, is not a moral and social panacea.

All too frequently Christian education is a matter of geography not philosophy. The philosophy, values and curriculum are often the same as that in public schools. The teaching is simply moved inside the four walls of a church.

The influence of teachers is also frequently overestimated. Young people surveyed almost always discounted the influence of teachers and emphasized the influence of their friends.[14]

A danger in Christian schools is to equate rules with religion. Those schools that maintain the dynamic of the Word of God will avoid this temptation. Rules administered with the spirit of Scripture are good discipline for a child and are not likely to generate rebellion. On the contrary, rules without biblical foundation or logic tend to generate rebellion.

Sometimes Christian schools are a gathering place for problem children. Many parents, believing the public school turned Johnny into a little monster, deposit him into the hands of a Christian school to make him a saint. His antisocial behavior and rebellion often are problems that distract the other children who want to learn.

The Christian school is at its best, however, when the staff and administration provide positive peer pressure. Ideally, the Christian school can support the Bible principles and values the parents have taught in the home. The Christian school can make one of its most positive contributions when it reflects Christian values, intelligence, and efficiency that is superior to the humanistic schools.

It should be noted that lack of discipline and restrictions placed on teachers in public schools has made it difficult for the education process to occur. The federal government, in an effort to provide "equal results" rather than "equal opportunity," has frequently disrupted the educational system.

MASSIVE PRESCHOOL CHILD-CARE PROGRAMS. The federal government has undertaken a patchwork of programs for preschool children. The theory that prompted the programs was that children need outside help in inner-city homes to maximize their early opportunities. The programs have failed because they treat symptoms, not causes. The parents must be changed, not the small children.

There is not a shred of evidence that either the behavior or the learning ability of children involved in the programs is permanently improved.

RELIGIOUS ISOLATION.   Social changes were observed by a variety of religious groups in this country. It was obvious that technology had something to do with changing values, so religious groups like the Amish refused to employ the new machines of modern America. In an effort to save their families' values they refused to drive automobiles, tractors, motorcycles, or employ other electrical or mechanical labor-saving devices.

Their efforts have failed because they misunderstood the relationship between technology and values. It is our response to technology that has disrupted family values and relationships, not technology itself. The young of the Amish are still leaving the farm in great numbers.

OPEN MARRIAGE.   Nena and George O'Neill in their book *Open Marriage* proposed that the problem with children and families in America was the burdensome requirements of the marriage contract. Ignoring absolute moral values, they suggested that the exclusive marriage relationship be abandoned and in its place a restyled type of monogomy, one adapted to contemporary realities. The O'Neills reasoned that the absence of limits, free sex, and freedom itself would make for quality relationships and well-adjusted children. The disasters of that experiment have demonstrated its shortcomings to most thinking people.

THE RELIGIOUS CULT.   Modern social developments that have accompanied the technological revolution with its dehumanization and fragmentation of the family have brought a longing for a sense of acceptance and community. Religious cults have flourished and are flourishing all over the nation. Estimates of those involved in them range as high as twenty million.

The cultists have offered themselves as substitutes for the family and its warmth. The young have been especially receptive. Cults have been able to rape the young of the nation emotionally and fanancially because of the void. *Commune* and *deprogramming* have only recently become a part of our common language. The cultists have agonized parents, further divided the country, and ripped off millions who looked for a place of belonging.

Vulnerability is so high that the cult leader does not need a highly developed system of thought or ideology. The decision to join is based on emotions and not rationality.

TESTED AND PROVED.   There has always been a voice for the biblical message of man's need for a Saviour. In the latter part of the last century that voice was Dwight L. Moody and in the early decades of the 1900s, Billy Sunday. The country was dotted with tents and brush arbors as well as churches where repentance for sins was proclaimed as necessary before faith in Christ could generate new spiritual life in the believer.

But gradually doubts crept into the very heart of the Christian church. Theologians became more concerned with higher criticism and the intellectual pursuits of doubts than in the redeeming love of Jesus. In the practical approach of the social gospel, humanism temptingly threatened man's dependence on God. The proclamation that God is dead, incredibly came not from an atheistic movement, but from modern theologians.

In reviewing the long history of the Judeo-Christian faith, there is a repetitive pattern that seems to be just as active today as in the days of Moses. The Israelites would disobey God's laws; in their rebellion, they would reject God, and because they were spiritual beings they substituted idol worship. Eventually, the natural consequences of their wanderings away from God brought them such pain, they would suddenly remember His love and care. A special leader would arise and help them to repentance, and, invariably, God would restore them. He often used people, but also intervened in miraculous ways to deliver them out of trouble. There would ensue a period of great peace and prosperity, until new generations arose who had forgotten the old situations. New drifting and rebellion would then arise, and the cycle was repeated.

Perhaps today's spiritual climate is parallel. As the focus of people was drawn to their pain in the depression and the war, they forgot God and searched for human answers. They found release from worry in escapism and security in materialism. Excitement became a substitute for joy, and sex for love. Power struggles replaced meekness, and license of hedonism removed the concept of temperance and self-control. Since man today is still a spiritual being, the vacuum of godlessness will be filled again with idols of hedonism or false cults such as Scientology, the Moonies, Hare Krishna, and occult religions. Satanism is no longer confined to the "heathen" countries, but has invaded various parts of our country.

Just as the Israelites exemplify the human tendency to backsliding, they also demonstrate the basic rules of returning. In his book *The Jews, God, and History,* Max Dimont examines the phenomenon of the Jewish people. Their very existence is miraculous. Jews, for centuries, have been a people without a homeland, scattered through virtually every culture on earth. Yet they have carefully and consistently maintained their national and religious identity. "They have had a continuous living history for four thousand years and have been an intellectual and spiritual force for three thousand years. They survived three thousand years without a country of their own, yet preserved their ethnic identity among alien cultures." [15]

They have been murdered, persecuted, maligned, and pressured to give up their Jewishness. Yet no culture nor ruler has been able to exterminate them. Hitler killed six million Jews. Those who survived emerged stronger than ever.

What is it that has enabled Jewish families to survive and insulate themselves from undesirable social pressures? The answer lies, at least partially, here:

> Now these are the commandments, the statutes, and the judgments,
> which the Lord your God commanded to teach you, that ye might do

them in the land whither ye go to possess it: That thou mightest fear
the Lord thy God, to keep all his statutes and his commandments,
which I command thee, thou, and thy son, and thy son's son, all the
days of thy life; and that thy days may be prolonged. Hear therefore,
O Israel, and observe to do it; that it may be well with thee, and that
ye may increase mightily, as the Lord God of thy fathers hath promised thee, in the land that floweth with milk and honey. Hear, O Israel:
the Lord our God is one Lord: And thou shalt love the Lord thy God
with all thine heart, and with all thy soul, and with all thy might. And
these words, which I command thee this day, shall be in thine heart:
And thou shalt teach them diligently unto thy children, and shalt talk
of them when thou sittest in thine house, and when thou walkest by
the way, and when thou liest down, and when thou risest up. And
thou shalt bind them for a sign upon thine hand, and they shall be as
frontlets between thine eyes. And thou shalt write them upon the
posts of thy house, and on thy gates.

                                                    Deuteronomy 6:1–9

This passage clearly assigns to the parents the responsibility for
teaching God's laws to their children and for training them to live
according to those laws. Not even to the religious leaders was this
sacred duty given.

Daniel is an example of a young man who resisted the pressure of
a godless culture. Theologians generally agree that Daniel was quite
young when he was taken as a captive from Judea to Babylon. We
are told nothing of his parents, but knowing the consistency of
Jewish traditions, we can imaginatively reconstruct his early years.

Until the age of six, his mother would have been responsible for
his care and training. At that age, his father would begin the religious teaching that culminated at thirteen in his bar mitzvah. This
ceremonious event celebrated a Jewish boy's transition to man-
hood.

Before Daniel's capture and eventual move to Babylon, his parents had trained him well. Perhaps Daniel was of royal descent since
he was chosen along with Shadrach, Meshach, and Abednego for
service to King Ahasuerus of Babylon. He was faced with extreme

pressure to conform to customs forbidden in his Hebrew faith. Daniel was served special food from the king's own table. This food was not allowed by his Old Testament laws. How hard it is to imagine that this mere boy, so alone and a thousand miles from home, risked antagonizing the king.

With dignity, courtesy, and respect, Daniel refused the king's food and was given the diet he requested. He must have earned the king's deep respect for he eventually became his advisor. Daniel's training had helped him develop a faith in God that brought about miraculous deliverances for him and his friends. It gave him courage to stand alone when he had to, because he knew what was right.

From ancient examples and honest modern thinkers, it seems clear that the family is the ultimate answer for the needs of children and the strengthening of our society. But these families must be strong and spiritually sound. They need sure plumb lines if they are to build homes that will survive social pressures. These guides are found in God's Word, the Bible. Honoring God and parents, respecting the person and property of others, honesty and integrity, are all summed up briefly in the Ten Commandments.

With the example and redemption of Jesus Christ and the promised power of God's Spirit, we are advantaged even beyond the power of the Old Testament. We can restore godly homes where mutual love and respect are the rule and where children can grow to healthy maturity.

Every family decision must now take on an added dimension. How will it affect the children? No job promotion, increase in salary, or added prestige is worth sacrificing a single child. Job transfers, increased hours, or added responsibilities are immoral if they adversely affect the children.

The modern corporation in the last three decades has required that men sell their bodies and souls to move up the corporate ladder. To salvage our homes and our children, we must be willing to give up the panelled board rooms, the plush country clubs, and even the cherished places on the corporate organizational charts.

Families must spend time together while the children are young. Television and other invasive influences must be controlled. It's not too late, but it will require courage, determination, and sacrifice to act to "save the children."

In the next chapters we will show the positive influences that lead toward developing normal, well-adjusted children. Rebellion *can* be prevented. However, in this society that is hostile to traditional values, conscious attention must be devoted to shaping the spiritual and psychological makeup of a child.

Chapter 3

The Building of a Child: Birth Through Preschool

Although there are similarities, your child does not, like Pavlov's dogs, respond with precision to ringing bells and mechanical devices. In contrast to the view of the humanist, the child is designed by God as body, soul, and spirit. Parents are responsible to train this child, but a sovereign God retains His control over the destiny of every child. Parents need to learn about the development of their children and how they can cooperate with God in the natural instinctive processes with which He has created them. They need, however, to avoid the current wave of hysteria that leads to harmful preoccupation with doing everything right.

There are certain time periods in a child's growth that can be cataloged to help us understand his normal development. With this awareness, parents can see the child's needs more clearly, meet them more adequately, and prevent serious rebellion later on. Each stage should be finished with a growing sense of trust, love, and good judgment. The developing child is thus enabled to face adulthood with excitement rather than futility, confidence instead of fear, and energy rather than the lethargy so common to the seventies. A natural growth away from the parents to independence can take place through this means. The ultimate goal of parenthood is to work one's self out of a job. The processes of the natural cleavage of child from parent are painful. The alternative, however, of a child's failure to be equipped to leave home is even more painful.

The initial stage includes the first two years of life. This most important period is the time of the initial and greatest separation of a child from his parents. The baby is crowded out of its cramped but securely dependent life in the mother's womb to a cold outside world that is not so safe. The welcome sound of a newborn baby's first cry is often due to the swat on the tiny bottom by the obstetrician.

In a world where fathers are so often left out, it is reassuring to see dads being included in the birthing of their children. Attending prenatal classes with their wives, coaching them through labor, and seeing the miraculous birth process, helps men to feel a part of their families in a significant manner. One father was so moved by sharing in the amazing process of the birth of his daughter, he experienced a new spiritual birth!

EARLY INDEPENDENCE.   At birth, an infant becomes physiologically independent—breathing on his own, taking in and digesting food, and eliminating the waste products of his metabolism. The providing of food, protection, and physical care of the baby must be done by his parents. The way the parent handles the child in the process of this care, creates a neurological imprint on his brain. In the remarkable masterpiece of the cycle of life, this earliest imprint initiates the eventual ability of the child to become a good parent. Infants treated with the gentleness of real strength, grow securely toward their next stage. Those who are abused or neglected, studies show, become, in turn, abusive parents. Recent statistics clearly indicate that 90 percent of parents who are child abusers were themselves abused as children.

During these impressionable two years, a remarkable degree of independence is achieved. The child who moves about only with twisting, purposeless motion at first, begins to walk by about one year. He identifies sights and sounds and learns to recognize familiar people.

GEOGRAPHIC LIMITS. The child's geographic limitations expand in proportion to his physical development and skills. He soon leaves the confines of the crib and playpen to explore the entire house. Parents who allow too much freedom at this time endanger a baby's life. Those who overprotect, endanger the growth of his curiosity and sense of confidence in himself.

A good guide for parents is the allowance of as much freedom to explore as the child's motor skills can safely handle. This requires close observation of the child's individual capability. Even at this early time, the parent should become aware that the natural processes of his child's development will result in eventual separation from him. There is normally pain in the knowledge that this time of cuddling and closeness will end. Accepting the necessity of this progressive cleavage will keep parents from the temptation of holding on to their children too long.

A girl of nine was a source of great concern to her public-school teacher. She was bright and physically normal, but she displayed all the characteristics of a very young child. She walked on tiptoe, spoke with the voice of a two-year-old, and was totally incapable of positive peer interaction. Investigation by the teacher led to professional counseling in search of the cause of this aberrant behavior. It was discovered that the child's mother would not permit the natural social growth of her daughter. In her unconscious need to keep the girl close and dependent, she had continued to treat her as a two-year-old. The girl's social and emotional development were arrested at that age. This is an example of damage done to a child by the parents holding on too long and too tightly. It is also typical of a parent who functioned out of her own needs rather than the needs of her child.

PHYSICAL DEVELOPMENT. From the early undirected movements of the infant, there is rapid development of motor skills. Babies sit up by six months and pull up and walk around the crib by nine or ten months. By twelve to fifteen months, mothers are excitedly calling grandparents to describe baby's first steps. Teeth are erupting, and eating habits as well as food preferences change.

There are wide variations in the time periods during which physical development takes place. Parents need to know only enough of this to prevent worry, but also to prevent problems due to neglect. Good medical checkups at regular intervals can provide peace of mind.

Eating and sleeping habits, toilet training, thumb sucking and infantile exploration of the genitalia can worry parents during these years. It is important that parents understand that each child's body knows how much he needs to eat and how long to sleep. Overreacting to these normal biological and physical processes can initiate needless battles that result in premature tensions between child and parents. Usually infantile thumb sucking and genital interest disappear as the child's interests and energy become directed outside himself and focus on other activities.

EMOTIONAL DEVELOPMENT. Each normal child is born with the potential for experiencing all the various emotions that make life so delightful. At birth most of these are embryonic, and only two are observable: anger and fear. Every mother will recognize that her precious, helpless baby is capable of fear! Just as she has rocked her child to sleep, the sudden barking of a dog or ringing of the telephone will produce a grasping movement of his arms, a look of surprise, and a loud cry that means she has it all to do over again. When a baby is hungry, wet, in pain, or bored, the reaction is different from that of fear. There is intense crying, the face turns red, and the entire body threshes about. Nearly all parents identify this as anger. From the baby's innate fear, come worry, anxiety, and other vulnerable feelings. Out of his anger, develop frustration, irritation, rage, and aggressive emotions. These emotions are natural defense mechanisms that gain parental attention to the child's needs.

Love develops in the child in response to love from the parents. As the child experiences love consistently, he learns to love others in turn. Fear demands reassurance that the child is being protected and cared for by the parent. This is an expression of love that even a tiny child understands. Ghosts, goblins, and wild animals fade away in the loving circle of a mother's arms. Sometimes tired parents, however, react to a child's fears with irritation or anger.

One young boy became convinced there were dangerous people in his backyard at night. Every sound was transformed by his childish fears into a serious threat to his safety. When he ran to his parents in terror, they ridiculed his fears and sent him back to bed comfortless. Left alone with his panic, he learned to feign physical pain to gain the attention he really needed for his fears.

How parents understand fear and anger in their child, determines their response. If they see these feelings as they are—an inborn means by which the nonverbal child can express needs and enter into a growing communication with his parents—they will respond with tenderness and protection. If, in contrast, they see fear as potential cowardice, or anger as future violence, or even as evidence of "inbred qin," they are likely to react with harshness. One father, for example, began to spank his babies at three months of age for crying out their needs. Obviously this father did not understand the nonverbal message of his children.

Parents must understand the three possible ways of dealing with feelings. The most damaging means is to repress them. For example, anger that is not permitted proper expression goes "underground." Over a period of time it is consciously forgotten. But, since anger is a real and inborn emotion, it will erupt; often later and in disguised ways that are confusing and destructive.

Many Christians see all anger as sinful. This is not scriptural. God was angry many times. Paul wrote, "Be ye angry, and sin not: let not the sun go down upon your wrath" (Ephesians 4:26). Expressing anger directly, with control, and using it to work out the problems that prompt it will prevent bitterness and hatred, which are wrong.

Let us elaborate on the matter of anger, specifically. Biologically, anger produces a response that can actually be measured. Anger stimulates the hormonal system to produce a substance called adrenalin. Its effect is to stimulate the body so that it is prepared to fight or run if these actions are necessary for protection. We have the power to decide if this energy will be used destructively or constructively. This power to choose and the control with which to exercise it must be taught to the child.

Pastor Dollar relates this story of a struggle over anger with one of his children:

> At the age of three, my youngest son engaged in temper tantrums when he failed to get his way. I refused to let his anger progress and become an uncontrollable part of his behavior. Each time his temper erupted, I would take him alone to the bedroom to deal with the problem. I would explain that uncontrolled anger would destroy him as an adult, and that he must learn to control it while he was young. I told him I didn't want him to grow up to be a ''brat.'' Each time I would ask him to tell me why he was being disciplined. Then I spanked him. After the spanking I asked him again to explain why he had been disciplined. Frequently, he would say, ''Because you don't want me to grow up to be a 'brat.' '' Then, to let him know I still loved him, I would wrap him in my arms and hold him as long as he wished. It took patience, but his anger was brought under control by love, not anger, on my part.

2) A second way people deal with feelings is to suppress them. In this method, feelings stay in one's awareness and are not forgotten. They are caged until they become so strong they may burst the bars with tragic results.

3) The third and best way to handle emotions is to express them, with control, in constructive and loving ways. Even anger can be extremely loving when it is expressed in this manner. (The authors would exclude a temper tantrum as a proper expression of anger.) Controlled anger includes understanding how one feels, why he feels that way, and what positive action he will take about it.

The repression of anger against a capricious parent is a form of emotional dishonesty. Righteous anger at injustice is real, and, when callously bottled up by a rigid parent, it will eventually explode in rebellion and sin. This concept can be taught even to young children by spiritual parents.

A fourteen-year-old girl had tried repeatedly to commit suicide. She could not explain the driving force within her that nearly destroyed her. One day, in desperate need of help for her, her foster parents called a counselor. Sally was visibly shaking as she sat with the therapist. The couch actually rattled beneath her. Unexpectedly, she recalled a scene from her past in which her father was beating her mother with a belt. Sally was three at the time. Standing and watching this terrifying incident, she screamed at her dad to stop hurting her mother, but he ignored her pleas. She felt so guilty about her fear and inability to help her mother that her childish mind could not take the pain. She had repressed this memory, but kept trying to hurt herself in a subconscious need to punish herself. After remembering this, she could understand that it was truly impossible for her to have stopped her father, and the guilt feeling was gone. She no longer needed to punish herself. Guilt feelings, like these, are very different from real guilt that results from willful wrongdoing.

The damage from suppression is illustrated by a recent story in a large city newspaper. A teenage boy lived alone with his divorced mother. He had been angry with her for leaving his father, and this anger grew year by year as she tried to raise him by cajoling, manipulating, or scolding him. He also loved her and appreciated her efforts to provide for him. For some years he held his anger in abeyance because he learned that he had more privileges when he did so. One day, however, the cage in which his anger lived broke open. His pent-up feelings, like those of a wild animal, caused him to stab his mother over and over, until she died. Only then did the wild anger return to its cage.

Dr. Ketterman relates this memory from her childhood:

> My father is a good example of expressing anger constructively and with proper controls. One spring evening, when I was only three, I lay in my crib while my big sister tried to sing me to sleep. I can still hear her soft voice as she sang, "G—double-o—d, Good, G—double-o—d, Good! I would be like Jesus, G—double-o—d, Good!" The old kerosene lamp glowed softly in the dark, and the song and love of my sister were all so soothing and warm. I was loving every bit of it and had no intention of sleeping. My sister had other things to do and felt I was ready to sleep. As she tiptoed softly from the room, I would open my eyes, cry loudly, and she patiently returned time after time for an encore. Finally, in desperation, she resorted to a higher

power. The response came in a strong male voice, my father's, saying, "Grace, if you don't quit crying, I'll come up and spank you!" Having no concept of a spanking, I decided it would be nice to have daddy join my party. With slight misgivings, I continued my game. After all, a child can't give up her power too readily.

Soon I heard a heavy tread up those stairs and down the hall. That sound wasn't like a partygoer's! Soon I learned several basic lessons: what a spanking was; that my father meant what he said; and that I had to relinquish some of my freedom in honoring the needs of others. Quite a teacher, my father!

SOCIAL DEVELOPMENT. Physically, geographically, and emotionally, the first two years are important in a child's development. The tiny baby cannot distinguish himself from his surroundings. He feels, as best we can explain, a part of his parents' arms, his crib, or whatever he touches. But very quickly, at least by three months, his eyes focus, he begins to move purposefully, and he soon discovers the difference in the "me" and "not me" parts of his world. He learns that his cry brings someone to his side to make him feel good. The baby soon discovers that he has some choice and power in gaining social relationships. If the adult who resonds is consistently kind and helpful, the child will develop trust and will learn to copy these loving ways. If most of the others in the child's world are warm and kind, this trust and love will spread in intermeshing circles to include the family, relatives, friends, and—later—the child's world in the community.

Without consistent kindness or with abuse, the child will need to test out other people in fear and suspicion. He will mimic the angry or abusive behavior and will probably grow into a rebellious teenager and an abusive parent himself. This learned behavior resembles that of angry, rebellious ways, but its early cause is different.

MENTAL DEVELOPMENT. The noted Swiss psychologist, Jean Piaget, found that intelligence is affected more by the kind of treatment the child receives in his first three months, than by inherited factors. If a new baby received much stimulation of his physical senses of sight, sound, movement, touch, and taste, he was likely to become a bright child, capable of learning. A child who was born with perfect genes and chromosomes, but who suffered neglect, might grow up almost as a retarded person.

Young children need to grow up in surroundings that stimulate their senses as well as satisfy them. Parents who teach children to smell and touch flowers, to feel the exquisite tickle of a fuzzy caterpillar crawling on their hands, and to sense the clean freshness of the wind blowing through their hair, are teaching them joy. Children who experience in nature the awe of this expression of God Himself do not have to resort to a search for hard, sophisticated excitement in their teens.

PERSONALITY DEVELOPMENT. ''The personality consists of habit patterns and qualities of behavior, as expressed by physical and mental activities and attitudes,'' so said Daniel Webster. Such a complex entity is influenced by many factors: the physical appearance and ability; the ability to love and trust; the curiosity to explore; the permission to be one's self; and many others. Family values and traditions influence expectations of a child and what is permitted in his behavior.

The personality is fairly well determined at eighteen months of age and quite set in a mold by three years. This means only the basic structure, of course, and changes take place throughout life that are influenced by our environment and life's experiences. By three, one can simply tell if a child will be shy or outgoing, intense or calm in his feelings, and aggressive or submissive by nature.

The shortness of the time in which parents can help a child to develop positive personality traits is frightening. Fortunately, it takes place early enough so that many years are left in which to enjoy the fruits of one's labors. When the early months are used constructively, a solid fundation will result. This makes successful teenage adjustments much more likely. In these days of the fragmented family and absentee parents, the significance of these early months cannot be overemphasized. Any vocational or social choices by parents should reflect their consideration of this fact.

SPIRITUAL DEVELOPMENT. Skeptics have endeavored to show that man's concepts of God are no more and no less than the child's extended concepts of his father. Our own experiences indicate that there are similarities. We see this, not as an argument against God, but as a verification of God's Plan. We believe God gave parents certain instincts for being good fathers and mothers. It stands to reason that these instincts would be patterned after God Himself, since He made man in His image. As parents treat their children, so do children come to see God. That is why one of the Ten Commandments, God's greatest moral coe for man, requires reverence for parents.

Dr. Ketterman tells of an appropriate story from her childhood:

> An example of this came to me recently from a friend who lived with my family when I was small. He described a favorite game I played with my father. He would perch me on a high place and tell me to jump into his arms. Eagerly I would leap from my precarious ledge, and he always caught me. I never questioned his strong arms or the loving spirit that consistently embraced me. It was relatively easy for me to take the spiritual leap, some years later, into the arms of the Father.

A thirteen-year-old girl, however, had an opposite story. She was admitted to a psychiatric hospital with serious emotional problems. One of her earliest memories was also of a game with her father. He would sit on the floor with his back against the wall and say, "Run to me, Judy!" She would run as fast as her chubby little legs could go. Sometimes he would catch her with a laughing embrace; but, at other times, he slipped adroitly aside at the last minute, and Judy would crash head-on into the wall. She remembered the pain and nosebleeds she suffered, but the joy of the times he was there kept her playing the game.

Fathers, you are a vital part of your child's idea of God. How do you portray Him? The jump into the loving, secure arms of an earthly father is not far from dependence upon a loving and reliable God.

Special Aspects of the Early Years

Congenital differences in temperaments are evident. Some babies are normally peaceful and easygoing. Others are energetic, extra sensitive, and react with intensity to very little stimuli. No one knows if this is genetically inherited, the result of biochemical factors, or a combination of both. Most mothers of two or more children have experienced this. Dr. Stella Chess conducted a study that extended over several decades and was based on observing the difference in temperament of a child and his mother. The results revealed significantly increased problems in many families where such differences occurred.

A mother, for example, who was quiet and needed a peaceful, orderly life was frustrated by a child who was energetic and loved to explore. Such a mother commonly tried to change this child by training or punishment, frustrating both mother and child. Fearing she was failing or that her child might be hyperactive, she would try harder, getting into battles and heroic efforts that ended in tears and resentments. Accepting the child as he is, setting reasonable limits with firm consistency, but not trying to change the cild's inborn temperament, will avoid many of these struggles.

There are three emotional needs that must be met in order to provide a positive climate for children. These three needs are affection, approval, and consistency. Affection must be unconditional. Parents, love and accept your children just because they exist, and because you choose to be loving and accepting. No one should have to earn love! Approval, however, does need to be earned. Approval is pride in the way a child acts or what he does. This requires discipline and help by the parents. Consistency is the quality that makes both affection and approval believable to the child.

Major failures in meeting any of these three needs will result in serious trouble later. Past studies by Dr. René Spitz revealed that little children had to have affection to stay alive. Certainly to maintain a healthy emotional life, we all must have unconditional love. Without love a child does not learn to love himself and without this, he cannot love others. Jesus made this so clear when He said, "Thou shalt love the Lord thy God with all thy heart, and with all thy soul, and with all thy mind," and "Thou shalt love thy neighbour as thyself" (Matthew 22:37, 39).

Approval is necessary for motivation. Many parents are deeply concerned these days about the lack of motivation in their children. Even in their twenties, many young people are content to work below their potential or not at all, and they allow their parents to support them. Upon investigation, many of these problems relate to the early years and a failure of the parents to express pride and approval in the child's little efforts at creativity and pleasing his parents. It takes time and energy to do activities with a child that seem useless or boring; but a child who is praised for stacking blocks or throwing a ball will work to stack them better and throw straighter. As this habit unfolds over the years, it leaves no room for lethargy. Approval requires discipline and the evaluation of individual skills. Letting a child get by with much less than his best and expecting more than he can possibly give are equally defeating in this process of motivating by approval.

Obedience is a quality in children that is discussed very rarely in today's literature. Recently, a group of kindergarten teachers were deeply concerned over a lack of obedience in five-year-olds. These youngsters frequently say, "I don't want to do that and you can't make me!" Indeed, an experienced teacher may not be able to force a child, even at age five, to do what he must do if he is to learn.

Consistency in discipline is necessary if a child is to learn obedience. One young mother, a musician, related this episode in the life of her first child.

Janie loved the bright, colorful covers of her mother's carefully cataloged sheet music and had, on one occasion, tasted it with disastrous results. Knowing it was time to teach her child to obey her, she took her to the area of the music and sat there with her and waited. Janie reached out her tiny hand to touch the bright paper and mother said, "No, Janie!" With only a short pause, Janie reached again. The stern voice commanded, "I said, 'No,' Janie!" Being a determined child, Janie reached out a third time, and this time her hand smarted from a firm swat. Janie cried with her mother, but, after a few repetitions of this ceremonious drama, Janie submitted.

The music was safe; but more importantly, Janie had learned obedience that would serve her well in all of her life. Her spirit was not broken, and she became neither depressed nor anxious. She did develop security in knowing where her limits were and being able to obey and live within them. She felt her parent's pride in her learning a valuable lesson.

Methods of discipline may vary according to the parent's wishes and the child's temperament and response. Old-fashioned spankings are still a valid means of discipline. Sitting a child on a chair or in a playpen, if he is younger, or even speaking in a stern voice may be enough to effect the needed obedience. The essential ingredients are careful watching, consistent enforcement of policies, and follow-through until each specific lesson is learned. In our stressful lives, it is tempting to let a child get by with disobedience when we are tired. But every time a parent allows this, it becomes harder to enforce the right behavior the next time.

A two-year-old girl was taken to a pediatrician's office because she had eaten an entire bottle of aspirins—enough to kill her. To save her life, she had to be restrained, and a large rubber tube was inserted in her stomach through her nose in order to remove these pills. During this painful and dramatic procedure, her mother casually commented, "This is the third time Debbie has done this in the last week." This mother had failed to set geographic boundaries for her child and had also failed to teach her to obey.

Preschoolers are capable of expanding their world geographically to the homes and yards of neighbors and friends. After three, if they have responded to good discipline with consideration for others, they can be trusted for short times out of the parents' sight. It is wise, however, for mothers to exchange reports with one another periodically in order to be sure of good behavior. Parents must keep an open mind regarding their child's actions and remember that he may act creditably and that he could also misbehave. There is a tendency on the part of some parents to blame all problems on the other child. Parents must not let their children's quarrels embroil the neighborhood.

PHYSICAL DEVELOPMENT. The two-year-old has, surprisingly, reached about half of his adult height. Growth and weight gains slow down and eating and sleeping habits are changing. Children commonly eat less and require much less sleep. Parents need not worry about this, but they should offer the child a reasonable variety of foods. Over a period of time, each child's body will stimulate his appetite for the type of food he needs. Fighting with a child over amounts and types of foods he must eat is useless and literally creates animosity and rebellion. It is imperative that obedience and consideration for others be taught; but body functions are instinctive and God-given, and interfering with them is simply not necessary.

Toilet training is possible between two and three, and this, too, need not be a struggle. Watching each child's individual signals of hunger, fatigue, and readiness for toilet training will enable parents to provide for these needs without battles. In the area of biological functions, flexibility within reason is wise!

EMOTIONAL DEVELOPMENT. The two-year-old may seem to be exclusively angry and stubborn. The repeated *no!* the recurring temper tantrums, and the continual resistance against authority are a miniature preview of possible teenage rebellion.

Temper tantrums are common at two, and often they express frustration and fatigue. Rarely, if ever, are they a deliberate attempt to give mothers a nervous breakdown. The toddler's body simply can't keep up with his mind or his wishes, and, in the naturally resulting frustration, his behavior breaks through his rudimentary controls.

Cures for tantrums range from ridiculous to dangerous. The best and most logical one is to pick up the kicking, screaming child and firmly but lovingly control him with your own body. He won't seriously hurt you if you wrap your arms and legs about him and hold him. Speak to him firmly but soothingly. Most children melt quickly into this welcome control and later will learn self-control.

Learning self-control is good for a lifetime. Giving in to a parent who is angrier than the child may be based only on fear, and often this turns to anger. Ignoring a tantrum seems to be the cruelest of all methods. The child who is so upset needs most desperately to be helped and protected, not ignored.

Fear is another common emotion from two to five. To deny the reality of fear or to see it as cowardice is to deny reality. Nightmares often awaken a child who is trying, even in his dreams, to resolve the struggles of his days. His own and his parents' anger explain much of the fear, though it expresses itself in many ways. One boy of three awakened nightly, screaming in terror. Turning on lights, rocking him to sleep at bedtime, soothing him when he awakened, did nothing to stop this nightly panic. "When all else fails, ask!" is a wise motto. Finally, his mother did ask, "Bobby, what scares you so?" He pointed a chubby finger at a poster of animals by his bed and replied with shaking voice, "Them tigers!" He had been disciplined with anger, and the ferocious-looking tigers were all too close to real life. Removing the poster helped, but his mother's gentleness and concern for his fears no doubt helped more.

Between two and five, children are comfortable in showing love. They give and receive affection with sincerity and energy. Parents need to take time to play with, rock, and cuddle their children at this age. Later on, they will reject such physical expressions, and they need to be saturated with them while they are responsive.

The preschool years are a good time to establish successful habits of clear emotional expression. When Helen Keller, blind and deaf as she was, learned to communicate, her unruly behavior changed quickly. At least by four, children can learn names for their feelings. They no longer need to act them out in sometimes frightening ways. The vocabulary of feelings must be taught, however. A very good way for this teaching to be done is by observation of the child. As some emotion is becoming apparent, the mother may say, for example, "Johnny, your face is getting red, and your voice is loud. You seem angry." She may have information to add such as, "I've noticed you get angry every time your little sister breaks up the nice things you build." A wise mother will understand: "I certainly don't blame you. I feel angry at interruptions, too!" She can teach him about solutions: "Why don't you let me know when Susie starts to bother you, or build up on the table where she can't reach." She may teach him to find his own good solutions by asking, "What can you do, Johnny, when you start to get mad at Susie?" To name the feeling, understand its origin, and find a solution for it takes care of most of the emotional problems of life for adults as well as children.

A shy child may need encouragement to express feelings and even teaching about how to do so. An intense child with easily aroused feelings, on the other hand, may need help in physically releasing some of the immediate tension before he can think through the logical steps listed above. For a young child, a pounding block is useful. For an older one, going to his bedroom and crying, or engaging in some acceptable form of physical exercise will burn up the surcharge of adrenalin.

SOCIAL DEVELOPMENT. There are a number of similarities between the two-year-old and the early adolescent. Some we have mentioned. Another is the no-man's-land in which both live for a time. The early toddler is not entirely dependent on the parent as he was, yet he is not able to cooperate in play with other children. Adolescents, in comparison, are neither children nor adults. The toddler typically does his own thing in the midst of others. He is more likely to fight over a toy than share it.

By ages three and four, most children have matured enough and gained an adequate sense of their own identity so that they can share and enjoy playing together with others. Parents and other adults who work with two- and three-year-olds need to understand this. Expecting good social skills too soon causes unnecessary anxiety and even rifts between parents and child. Children under three, for example,

probably are more secure with their own mother or a baby-sitter
with one or two other children. Day-care centers are tempting con-
veniences, but few are equipped to deal with a roomful of two-year-
olds. Socially, the four- and five-year old is quite skilled. He will use
the patterns of relating and communicating that he has formed within
the family. Watching a preschooler play house or interact in a group
will reveal a caricature of his own family.

The child who has learned to manipulate mom against dad in order
to get his way at home will use the same techinque between parents
and neighbors or teachers. To promote good social adjustment,
adults need to intervene as little as possible in the usual quarrels of
children. They must not take sides and need to focus carefully on
what is right and not who is right.

MENTAL DEVELOPMENT.   The development of a vocabulary makes
learning increasingly fun for children and parents. Most toddlers
love to share books with their parents. They develop such preferences for certain ones, that parents are bored with the endless repetition of *Goldilocks* or *Peter Rabbit*. But repetition is a time-honored
method of learning. As a child learns the story, he senses the value
of learning itself. Many children with learning disabilities have not
had parents read to them for fun. Some have been pressured to learn
to read too early and rebel against this. It is usual that early emphasis on learning skills is for the parents' egos and not the child's
good. Observing each child's interest and readiness for exploring
new areas of learning is the only safe guide for teaching him.

The continuation of teaching children to enjoy their physical
senses is important. The integration of all phases of learning by
experiencing is stimulating to their curiosity and their mental
growth.

A child of this age span is capable of making limited choices. The
ability to reason and make wise decisions can be developed at this
early age. Offering a child one of two possible choices, neither of
which could be harmful, will teach him respect and healthy self-
confidence. Simple, positive comments about the choice he made
will encourage growth in good decision making. The young person of

eighteen is not abruptly capable of making independent, wise choices. That process is learned and trained over the whole span of his previous life. This process does not suggest an abdication of parental authority. The parent maintains and expresses his authority by his careful selection of safe, alternate choices. This policy by the parents involves the calculated risk of mistakes by the child. It is through such mistakes that the parent has opportunity to guide and teach the child to make even wiser choices the next time.

Explanations are important to a child's developing understanding, and they are especially useful with the adaptable preschooler. Taking time to explain the reasons for expectations or disciplinary measures helps the parent form habits of fairness and respect for the child. More than likely, it will gain the child's cooperation and respect for the parent. Certainly there are strong-willed children who will not accept explanations, and firmer measures will have to be used at times; but, when it works, reasoning will promote a positive, warm relationship between parent and child.

PERSONALITY TRAITS OF THE TWO- TO FIVE-YEAR-OLD. Besides gaining some awareness of his personal power and his limits, the main quality of personality development during these years is that of creativity. Children at this time are capable of imagining delightful things and playing them out in unique ways. This sense of initiative needs to be encouraged. Displaying childish projects and works of art for family and friends to enjoy is a sure means of teaching a child the value of his inventiveness. In the necessary regimentation of later life, many children lose this individual creative ability.

Childish imaginations are part of creativity and should be enjoyed with the child. Be careful to separate the *pretend* from the *real*. It is especially important that the child be kept from wishing angry or harmful things. Occasionally real tragedies happen coincidentally with an angry wish, and the child may believe his wishes magically caused it. A horrifying sense of guilt and power may settle on such a child and torment him for years.

Television, unfortunately, has become an archenemy of creativity. By spoon-feeding its quick flicks of excitement, it has displaced in our attention the originality, creativity, and imagination that stimulate personal growth. Not even in stage plays or movies is there the harm of the bombardment of violence and excessive stimulation of television. Parents must be aware and in charge of television in their homes. A misguided reaction to the harmful effects of television on the child is to eliminate the television totally. This solution removes the learning experience of making choices and also ignores the positive benefits that come from selective viewing with parental supervision. Constructive use of television is possible, for example, by discussing what is shown and by teaching children the misconceptions portrayed. This takes energy, time, and creative thinking by the parents.

Creativity must be cultivated in order to grow in a child. Each person in a family is different and needs to be observed closely to find his unique abilities. Parents need to supervise the child enough to see to it that he consistently does his individual best. They need to crown the effort with honest, unqualified praise. Someone has said that the parents of the last twenty-five years are the "Yes, but . . ." generation of parents. We have dutifully accepted our task of encouraging skills by finding fault. By mixing praise and criticism, we have, at best, confused our kids and, at worst, utterly discouraged them. Many children hear, "That's nice; but why did you miss that?" What they need to hear is "Repeat that job to your best ability, Jim"; and then, "Jim, that's great! Let me tell you what's good about it."

Two high-school-junior debaters consistently won in preliminary rounds of debate, advancing to elimination rounds. Week after week, on the debate circuit, they returned to parents anxiously awaiting their results. The boys were meeting some of the stiffest competition in high-school-debating circles. Although doing extremely well, they returned each week with only a second- or third-place trophy. A disgusted, but misguided, father, seeing yet another second-place trophy, exclaimed, "Can't you boys ever win first place?"

SPIRITUAL DEVELOPMENT. The preschooler can understand much about God, especially through nature. The wonder in a child's eyes when he sees a star, a flower, a bug, or a kitten is an exquisite validation of the natural faith of a child. When parents take time to share in this wonder and to teach even more, there is a cementing together of the love and joy of life. Paradoxically, this kind of intimacy produces the security that makes releasing the child later on much easier. When parents can transfer the hand of their child to that of the Heavenly Father, it's not so hard to let go.

Here, Dr. Ketterman illustrates this:

> The wisdom of God is still pictured for me in a memory of my early childhood. One warm spring day my father took me by the hand and led me to the chicken house. A twinkle in his eyes told me this was to be an exciting surprise. And it was! He led me to the place where tiny baby chicks were laboriously pecking their way out of the shells that had housed them for three weeks. They worked away vigorously with tiny yellow beaks for a while and then stopped in exhaustion. In my childish compassion and eagerness, I knew they needed help. I asked my dad if I could pick off some of the shells for them. He explained that I must not do that because the chicks could grow strong enough to live outside the shell only if they exercised in this strenuous way. He told me that God had made the animals perfectly so they knew just what to do. Having learned obedience already, I waited and watched. Dad was right. I learned to believe.

SEXUAL DEVELOPMENT. Preschoolers usually have many questions that relate to sexuality. They wonder about their own bodies and how they differ from those of their brothers or sisters. They wonder where babies come from and are aware of baby animals. Sometimes, playmates explore each other's bodies. This sexual awareness troubles many parents. They feel embarrassed and don't know how to respond. They may scold or shame a child for a very natural curiosity. Actually, preschoolers want very simple answers and not long lectures on biology.

A farmer told this wonderful story. His daughter had asked him a number of questions about baby lambs and how they were born. He explained to her as honestly and simply as he could about their birth process. One cold winter evening he was busily helping a mother ewe bear her lamb. Looking up he saw the wide-eyed wonder in the face of his child as she was intently inspecting the process from the barn door. She smiled a lovely smile as she said, "Daddy, it's exactly like you told me." This girl had no need to hide her curiosity and learn from pornography or dirty stories. Her source of information was safe and reliable.

The preschool child goes through a sexually significant experience. It is typical that a little boy who loves his mother fancies sooner or later that he will grow up and marry her. He protects her in amazing ways, especially during arguments between his mother and father. One little boy of three took the toy gun out of his cowboy holster and threatened to shoot his daddy if he was cross with his mother.

Little girls, similarly, believe they will some day marry their daddies and live happily ever after. This is a normal experience and begins to prepare the child for real courtship and marriage much later. Most adults marry someone like one of their parents.

During this time a child needs time with and approval from the parent of the opposite sex in order to establish a positive sexual identity. Each child requires this time and, with it, the blessing of the other parent in order to avoid shame or guilt. If one parent becomes too permissive or allows the child to manipulate him or her, the other may become resentful. Unless parents work carefully through this time, the child will become a pawn over whom they compete and argue. Mothers and fathers must stay first in each other's love and respect, with the children loved and shared equally in their affections. This period of psychosexual development is relatively short in duration. Parents need not be anxious nor overreactive.

"There is no perfect parent or no perfect child."

Chapter 4

The Building of a Child: Kindergarten Through Adolescence

It is a strange, even terrifying, new world that a child faces when he first enters school. Until that time, the parent has had maximum control over a child's activities and development. The separation, which comes upon a child's entering school, represents the end of a major era of a child's life. For both parent and child it is often accompanied by grief and doubt. Although a major part of the life print has already been etched, the process is by no means complete or irrevocable. The caring parent moves into a new phase of refining and building upon foundations already laid. This untried era involves cooperation with new forces outside the home that will add to the molding of the child. Some of these forces may be hostile and stimulate fear in the child. While generally cooperating with school authorities, parents need to recognize threatening areas and offer protection to the child.

time span   1st — 6th grade

Preadolescence (Six to Twelve Years)

The elementary schoolchild grows slowly. He learns academic skills and how to get along with people outside his own home. He usually is learning fundamental skills in sports, music, or other areas of creativity.

91

PHYSICAL DEVELOPMENT. School-age children have achieved the foundation of their muscular development. They are capable of fine motor skills such as coloring or painting, as well as gross motor skills used in athletics. Practice is important, and at this crucial stage of development children whose parents spend time encouraging them in areas of special skills and interests will generally do well.

Physical problems at this time are usually few. Typical childhood diseases are over or have been prevented by immunizations. Anxiety over social or academic problems may cause somatic symptoms. Frequently schoolchildren suffer headaches or stomachaches. Sometimes nightmares, similar to those of the two-year-old, come back and are signs of stress that is too hard for the child to manage. These are usually transient, and parents need not be alarmed unless they last over a period of several weeks.

Children often manifest stress through the appearance of tics. These are facial grimaces or other involuntary body movements. They begin as a reflex reaction to a stress such as fear or surprise, but become habitual and often uncontrollable. They are irritating to observers, and concerned parents frequently ask the child to stop.

Often a self-perpetuating emotional and physical cycle begins. The child's tic annoys the parent; the parent scolds the child; the child feels more anxious; the tic accelerates; and the parent becomes more annoyed. The cycle is completed. If parents will ignore the tic, remove some of the stress on the child, and give him extra love and support, he will generally overcome this habit.

The pituitary gland in the base of the skull, the thyroid, adrenal, and sex glands are very slowly accelerating the growth and sexual development. As early as eight or nine, breast tissue may begin to develop in both boys and girls. Boys and parents may be alarmed unless they know this is normal, and it will disappear as the hormones balance out. By ten or eleven, body hair begins to grow, and the body contours and proportions begin to change to those of the young adult. Girls seem to mature in most ways prior to boys.

Freud called this the "latency period," and he believed that children at this age were unaware of sexuality. If only that were true! Children need to concentrate their life energy in play, learning, and creativity of all kinds. In today's world, however, children of five and six are focusing fairly intently on more mature sexual concerns. Kindergartners know as much about homosexuality as college students once knew. By second or third grades, many children are preoccupied with boyfriends and girl friends to the extent of kissing, adult-sounding phone calls, and serious anxiety about being accepted or rejected. The mass media emphasize sex so much that six-year-old girls beg to wear bras, and girls of ten or eleven are in anguish if they are flat-chested!

The authors believe that the home is the ideal framework for good sex education. Parents and children need to be able to discuss sexual matters openly and appropriately as the interest and need of the child arise. Neither sex nor sex education is sinful, but the proper climate of morality and responsibility is needed to avoid hedonism. Parents and teachers need to cooperate to discourage such sexual preoccupation. They should not tease children about these concerns. Instead they need to encourage the freedom to play with boys and girls alike in healthy games and competition. Such physical skills as may be developed in these ways will provide opportunity for social interaction through life.

They must have limitations

GEOGRAPHIC BOUNDARIES. Children of school age are increasingly capable of exploring their entire communities with some independence. They usually can walk or bicycle to school alone or with friends. They can make limited purchases in local stores and can be responsible for meeting time schedules. Time alone in large shopping centers or loitering about stores, however, is dangerous. Temptations to shoplift or accept drugs are ever present.

Even public parks in urban areas are no longer safe for unattended children. Parents and teachers are hard pressed to encourage the needed independence and yet insure adequate protection to the child.

EMOTIONAL DEVELOPMENT. Children, in today's confusing world, are subject to intense emotional pressures. Even young children become depressed and—in increasing numbers—have been known to commit suicide. They often are worried about failure, especially in their parents' eyes, and in the later grades are anxious about peer approval. Even the usual quarrels between mothers and dads may cause anxiety about a possible divorce since many of their friends have known parental separation. Christian families are rarely exceptions to such concerns. School phobias are fairly common and usually are due to problems about family matters rather than school difficulties. *must be directed toward that which is ev*

Anger may settle into hostility and defiance at this young age. The feeling that no one understands becomes fixed. Early in their school life many children have experienced repeated failures until a failure pattern has become fixed. Some children never recover. Unless there are areas of success and real fun to compensate for their burdens, children may be ripe for drug or alcohol abuse by the age of nine or ten.

. This is the best opportunity—and nearly the last—to teach children to recognize and handle their feelings of love, vulnerability, or aggression. Parents urgently need to be available, understanding, and firm but kind regarding the child's emotionality. They need to permit and even encourage the child to talk out his feelings. Being a *real* person is to know what one feels, say so appropriately, and be so honest about it that one's facial expression, gestures, and posture confirm it. People often say the proper courteous words, but their faces look angry. They may have a smile on their lips, but tears in their eyes. It is hard for the other person to know which feeling is real. We can teach children to be genuine in putting together their actions, words, and feelings. Doing so prevents misunderstandings and permits prompt healing of unintended hurts!

The child of school age is confronted for the first time with new and frightening authority figures. Teachers and principals speak with godlike authority in the opinion of little children. These youngsters are often terrorized by teachers who are unwittingly insensitive to their feelings.

This fear often prompts an extreme effort to please the teacher by conforming to every detail of his authoritarian edicts. Though this fear may appear irrational or even humorous to an insensitive parent, it is very real to the child.

A parent reported this story of fear in his second-grade son. The son asked his mother to provide a note to his teacher explaining his absence from class. The boy insisted that the note be on pink paper. The mother, having no pink paper, was puzzled and annoyed and began to write the note on white paper. Her son, now in tears, insisted that it had to be on pink paper. He was so distraught over having a note that was not pink, that he resisted going to school the next morning. The still-perplexed mother knew it was wise to inquire about such an unreasonable-sounding rule. She learned from the teacher that a commonly used term by teachers to gain permission for errands was "pink slip." The child had wrongly inferred that all communications must be on pink paper. Though his fears seemed unfounded, the boy needed comfort and reason, not scolding or ridicule.

Children's fears are also prompted by misunderstood words used by authority figures. Young children think very literally while adults commonly use figurative language. Many school districts have learned that it is almost impossible to successfully move a high-school teacher to an elementary school. Their figurative language is frequently misinterpreted and may even frighten a highly sensitive child.

A teacher may say, "If you move out of your seat, I'll break your arm!" The use of this phrase is symbolic, but the teacher may never understand that the youngster actually believes his arm might by broken.

PROGRESS TOWARD INDEPENDENCE. The natural parent-child separation is moving more rapidly by the late grade-school years. Many elementary-school children get up alone, fix their own breakfast, get ready, and go to school by themselves. To those of us who were accustomed to a parent's attention and wishing for us a "good day," this seems sad. Many children return to empty homes to the care of the "one-eyed sitter." They await their parents' return for a quick-food dinner and often are left alone again as parents pursue other activities.

Such children have so much freedom and so few limits, they literally have nothing against which to rebel. They constantly look for limits and for someone to care. They do find a range of resources: a gang of older kids will take them in for a price; they may find comfort in pills or alcohol from friends or their parents' cupboards; or they may build a layered shell of callouses from their hurts where the pain of loneliness can no longer penetrate. What they need is quality time with a caring adult who enjoys them.

While such independence is possible, it is not desirable. Children still need a parent to be available for needs or simply as a friend.

SOCIAL DEVELOPMENT.   Healthy school children play in groups regardless of age or sex. Their best social activities are intense physical ones. Competitive games are excellent, but there needs to be a fair chance for everyone to win at something. In today's overly crowded schools and highly competitive childhood sports programs, too few can even play, much less win! Losing may become such a habit that even the usual sense of sadness is gone after a while, leaving only a numb indifference.

Watching children walk through the halls of a crowded school is revealing. So many are sad-eyed as they walk, unnoticed, through monotonous days with no more hope, or even effort, for recognition. Maybe it is the stronger ones who rebel—who disobey in order to be noticed at least!

Loneliness is not the absence of people, but the absence of relationships. The loneliness of homes combined with an impersonal school tends to produce despair in the child. In an effort to increase efficiency and reduce costs, schools districts have consolidated into massive and impersonal institutions. In urban America, the warmth of individualization has been almost lost within many schools. A child who is uninvolved with his teacher is more likely to be influenced by his peers. More than 89 percent of children interviewed in our survey who made such a choice stated that they were influenced more strongly by peers than by teachers.[1]

Many children, unfortunately, extend their need to compete into social arenas where they belittle others in order to get in with the popular crowd. Children quickly learn the artificial smile and the sometimes dishonest compliments that may make them leaders or at least buddies of the leaders. By the close of the grade-school era, there are few children who have the security and the positive self-regard that enable them to resist such social games. This tendency to artificiality is then supported in adult life by popular, success-motivational literature.

MENTAL DEVELOPMENT.   Mentally, grade-schoolers are building the superstructure on their preschool foundation. They will build academic excellence, mediocrity, or failure, depending on the sort of foundation they have. When early parenting has been inadequate or when home and family problems fill their minds with anxiety, children cannot focus on modern math or reading. We have seen many children with normal mentality failing in school because of such worries.

Teamwork between parents and teachers is essential to optimum mental growth. This, unfortunately, is hard to achieve, and teachers and parents tend to take adversary roles. You see, parents want most intensely to be good parents. The proof of good parenting, obviously, is in the product—a fine, successful child. If the product is less, it must be the fault of someone else and, in the school years, who is more logical to blame than the teacher? Teachers, in turn, want intensely to be good teachers, and the evidence of their success lies in that of their students. So, when a student is not doing well, especially if the others in class are achieving, then the fault must be the parents'!

Laying aside the doubt and fear of one another and becoming a team working with the child can change school failure to success. Finding each child's best potential for success takes cooperation and time. Helping him realize this potential is work. But once he experiences success, with the rewards of praise and his own sense of pride, most children will grow in both motivation and accomplishment.

Perhaps the most serious deficiency in the life of a child is the absence of adult involvement with his struggles. Maybe some day a vocational school for children will be built that concerns itself with discovering individual abilities and creating pride in those talents, no matter whether they are street cleaning or engineering. Failure is giving up or falling below one's best through indifference.

PERSONALITY DEVELOPMENT. During the school years, a vital ingredient must be added to the child's personality. This component is a sense of duty or responsibility, and it is badly needed if we are to keep our culture livable. Before schooling begins, the foundations for this quality need to have been built. It centers around the ability to love and trust, a sense of one's strength and importance, and the development of creativity. These are all important if the older child is to see the possibility of becoming responsible during these school years.

A sense of responsibility is essential to success in all areas of a child's life. Being able to accomplish school work without constant reminding depends on this ingredient. An awareness of others' needs and rights demands a sense of responsibility in choosing to give up some freedom in order to give others their rights. This sense is necessary also in learning to work independently and cooperatively in a group; it is essential for fair play and teamwork.

Human nature being what it is, teaching responsibility to children requires constant care and input! Dr. Ketterman tells another story about her childhood.

One night in October when I was barely nine, I was in bed and soundly asleep when I heard my name called, emphatically, by my father. In my sleepy thoughts I could not imagine why he wanted me out of bed and downstairs at 9:30 at night when he had just demanded I stop my favorite pastime of reading to go to bed. His reason was soon quite clear. After school I had several jobs to do. These were exclusively mine and no one else did them, unless I conveniently forgot them in order to give preference to my precious reading. How often someone else had done my jobs, I don't recall. I am quite sure, however, that no one ever did this job for me again, because my father demanded my going outside in the dark, alone, to do it. There were coyotes out there, and I didn't like being alone with them! The only logical future choice was to do that job when it was light and other people were around. It would have been easier for Dad to do this job than to get me up, listen to my complaints, and know my fright. But he cared enough for me to take the hard route.

Unless parents or teachers care that much, children will miss out on an essential ingredient in their lives. And careless children grow up to become irresponsible adults.

SPIRITUAL DEVELOPMENT. Important spiritual choices are almost invariably made by children during this age span. The Catholic church allows children of seven to receive the sacraments of Penance and the Eucharist, and it believes they are capable of understanding enough to make a commitment to their faith. A modern-day school of psychology affirms that most of one's life-determining decisions are made by age eight. Other Christian churches agree that relatively few people make a commitment to Christ for the first time after they are twelve. For a child to make this significant life choice, three things are required: (1) a positive approach in teaching spiritual principles; (2) consistency in the example of the teachers' lives; and (3) an opportunity and invitation to crystalize such a decision.

There is power and personal guidance in prayer. It is an act of faith, when a parent has done the best job he can in teaching his child, to commit the child to God through prayer. Like the mother of Moses who, in obedience to a loving God, released her son in a tiny ark on the forbidding Nile, we must release each child to the Heavenly Father.

Puberty

Next to birth and the change of life in a person, puberty is the most profound physical change during the course of a lifetime. Although the changes during puberty are seen most obviously in the physical body, there are dramatic changes in virtually every area of life. Adolescence caps all the prior developmental stages and is the final gateway to the adult world. If serious rebellion invades adolescence, the adult life may be permanently marred. The significance of this age is verified by the authors' survey. It was determined that the average age at which these young people first seriously questioned the moral value system of their fathers was 11.3 years.[2]

BIOLOGICAL CHANGE.   A tiny, round mass about the size of a pea at the base of the skull, the pituitary gland, increases its secretion of powerful growth hormones into the body at about age twelve. This change occurs in both boys and girls.

The same gland that pumps oxytocin into the body of a mother to start contractions at the birth of her child secretes other hormones that determine the height of the body and regulate the aging process. It is in fact the "master" gland that is involved with the functioning of all of the endocrine glands in a complex interactional fashion. The thyroid and adrenal glands, ovaries, and testicles are all parts of this intricate system.

It is a strange and disturbing event when a child enters puberty. Growth hormones make striking changes that begin the process of turning a child into an adult. There is a sudden spurt of growth. It is not uncommon for some boys to grow four inches in one year. In girls, the menstrual cycle begins and the mammary glands develop. In both boys and girls, pubic and axillary hair begin to appear, and boys develop facial hair. A stirring in the body begins as adult sexual impulses develop. Almost overnight a thirteen-year-old child has entered a new world as she and he develop the capacity to conceive and bear children.

A major change, unfortunately, that needs to take place at puberty may get out of balance and create mutual pain for parent and child. As the child develops secondary sexual characteristics, there is a sudden reaching for privacy, and even a demand for isolation may take place. The earlier attraction between the child and the parent of the opposite sex is vaguely stirred, and often there is an overreaction to this. The universal, unspoken, primitive tabu against incestual urges goes into effect.

As a child reaches almost adult sexual maturity, a change in his relationship with the parent may take place. The old childhood feelings and fantasies for the parent are briefly revived. A father who has held his little girl tenderly on his lap develops a new sense of discomfort at holding her close. Her body contours and her behavior are so similar to his sexual mate, that there is confusion for a time in his feelings. Some parents react to this discomforting feeling by pulling away from the child and avoiding such contact. The child feels rejected and confused at this sudden change.

Parents need to remember the unique instinctive type of love with which God endowed them—the agape love of protective and nurturing qualities that they knew when this child was born. While awareness of the new adult sexuality is there, this can be treated with dignity and respect, not fear or embarrassment. The new and untried feelings of the child can indeed be drawn under the umbrella of the agape love, and both the child and parent helped to accept, value, and control them as he or she has learned to do with other emotions earlier.

Geographically, the world is indeed the limit as young people can now travel almost anywhere by hitchhiking and "locking-in" with other people. People whose life-style is indifferent to family values will shelter rebellious teens in incredible fashion. There is a "Do-your-own-thing" philosophy that somehow justifies license among all people—a possible precursor to anarchy that presages a real danger to our civilization.

THE EMOTIONAL CHANGES. The feelings of the adolescent are characterized by confusion. At times the early teenager would rather revert to early dependency. Alternately, he is ready to be independent. Since the youth is uncertain each day about which world he wants to live in, his behavior fluctuates from maturity to childishness. Parents who live with such behavior are themselves often confused in determining appropriate responses. Patience and understanding are essential to both child and parent through this uncomfortable period.

In response to their bodily changes, adolescents in our culture begin to demand privacy. Girls and boys begin both closing and locking doors while they dress. Children during adolescence increasingly exercise their territorial rights. In their own minds they mark off a section of the home that they believe to be their exclusive domain. For the first time, brothers and sisters as well as parents are told, "Stay out of my room."

A new awareness of personal ownership emerges that does not resemble the quarrels of younger years over "my toy." A sense of ownership—almost a legal sense—develops. Although it is still "our house," it becomes "my radio" and "my dress." Often, this is concerned more with an underlying power struggle or a testing out of fancied parental partiality than it is a need for ownership per se.

The child at puberty has a new sense of awareness of his physical and emotional being. He focuses upon it in an intense manner. Some children develop a strong sense of their own significance. It is not infrequent that an adolescent feels that he is, in fact, at the epicenter of all the universe. This is a natural expression of the immensity of his transition from the child to the adult world. It is probable that in addition to his new physical awakening, a new spiritual awareness is emerging. At this juncture, he may see himself for the first time as a unique creation of God.

THE SOCIAL CHANGES.   At puberty a child's progressing maturity enables him to attend more activities away from the home. This mobility creates a whole new social world for the child. New and closer friends are a natural outgrowth of this freedom.

Family values are now tested against those of friends, and today's permissiveness seems desirable to the teen who is struggling for his own freedom. The need for the approval of friends has been growing for several years. It now becomes, for many, a driving force that transcends the old wish for parental approval, though this is still present. The teen often wants—and usually needs—his parents to stand firm on issues even against his pleas. He needs the parents to be "square" for him, until he is mature enough to take the derision from his peers that such a stanj might create. The parents vicariously take the blame for the child.

A new type of peer relationship brings painful social dilemmas and adjustments. Experimental and tentative friendships develop, and a whole new vocabulary emerges to describe them. The words and phrases change from generation to generation, but they describe the same things. Boys and girls are "going steady" and the expression "girl friend" means more than a female friend.

THE INTELLECTUAL CHANGES. It is certainly possible for children to think in abstractions before puberty. This type of thinking, however, begins to play a more dominant role in the adolescent's mind. Idealism, patriotism, loyalty, school spirit, and prejudice have been a part of the child's vocabulary. These terms now take on deeper meanings. Learning and study habits, preparatory for college and a successful career, are being developed at this time. Permissiveness has invaded the academic world, and teens are allowed with increasing freedom to choose subjects of special interest to them. The freedom to choose only easy or interesting subjects prevents the pain of boredom. It does not, however, expose the young person to the challenge of more difficult pursuits nor grant him the thrill of achievement. The excitement of the intellectual conquest of more may be missed. Ours is a world which values *ease,* and through this philosophy we can lose the strength of character that enables survival in adversity. In the pursuit of the adolescent's mental development, school authorities and parents need to collaborate to keep alive the challenging of fine, but sometimes lazy, young minds.

Teens love to argue and disagree with one another and especially with adults. Parents often panic at this and see it as evidence that they have somehow failed, and their offspring are discarding all of their tried and tested values. In their very fear, they overreact and try harder to make the child see adult values as the ones that are right. The parent wants, in a final desperate thrust of parenting, to force the child into his own mold so he will know the child can make it and his own values will not be threatened.

This is self-defeating! The parent may rest securely in having done the best job that he could possibly do a day at a time; in having loved, gently and firmly, each child as best he could; in teaching and living, as clearly as possible, what seemed right. It is certain that the parent has made mistakes. Asking forgiveness of the child for a parent's past mistakes will clear away old resentments. He may know these specifically and constructively discuss them with the child. But now the child, as the parent once did, must forge ahead largely on his own. He must forgive his parents' mistakes as he is forgiven through understanding.

Disagreements and independent thinking, therefore, are to be encouraged as evidence of the parents' success and healthy maturity of the child. When parents can adopt this philosophy and accept their teenagers as intellectual equals, a mutual respect will emerge. Often an honest parent will find himself learning from his own offspring! Certainly, when this respect is felt, the doors of communication will stay open, and the teen will see the parent for what he will be perhaps from now on—a place of returning for the wisdom of age, the unconditional acceptance of love, and the expression of pride and approval for efforts well made.

Chapter 5

What Went Wrong in the Home?

"It happened so suddenly. Everything seemed fine, then one day Kent rebelled. He turned into a different person." Parents have said it over and over, but it is not true. Unless there is a physical illness that causes irrational behavior, rebellion almost never develops suddenly. It may be well disguised, and even caring parents may fail to see the signs, but rebellion is a process, not an incident. The growth of rebellion is often a long, almost imperceptible process, that can take years to develop into a serious gulf between parent and child.

He had been out of high school only two weeks. His mother noticed that he was not dressing for church and would make the family late. When questioned, he quietly, almost apologetically, informed both of his parents that he would not be attending church with them anymore. He was nineteen years old and had missed few Sundays in his life. To his parents it seemed abrupt; but, when questioned, his secret doubts and rejection of their values and theology went back to the ninth grade. At sixteen, the arguments of Nietzsche had penetrated his long-established belief in a personal God. When he came for counseling at eighteen, he was still hurting from the fresh pain he had caused his parents by his revelation of his inner beliefs; but, his feelings were not new. They were deep and painfully long in their growth.

The rebellious child is, generally speaking, a normal child being raised through a natural process that goes wrong. We do not know a lot about cancer; but we do know that, in the natural process of development, cells begin to multiply more rapidly than normal. Soon the natural cellular-multiplication process is out of control; and a normal-growth process, gone awry, becomes deadly.

In the confusion of modern language with all of its shades of meaning, *Webster's Dictionary* is most useful. In its definition of *rebellion* we are reminded of the old Latin root words *re* meaning "again" and *bellare* meaning "to wage war." Put together, these words tell us that rebellion is "to wage war again." Indeed that is what families experience in dealing with a rebellious member—the waging of open warfare between two sides—again and again. The defiance, anger, and hurt of this war are immeasurable.

Rebellion is not always predictable. Even in the same home, one child may be emotionally healthy and loving toward parents while another completely rejects parental authority and values. It would be wonderful if a nice, neat little formula could be devised for parents that would guarantee saintly, devoted children. The complexities and variables in children and child rearing make that impossible; however, there are parent-child relationships and pressures that are more likely to create problems for certain children. Arlene Skolnick, a research psychologist at the Institute of Human Development in Berkeley, California, agrees that there are no pat answers. She has stated, "Popular and professional knowledge does not seem to have made parenting easier. On the contrary, the insights and guidelines provided by the experts seem to have made parents more anxious. Since modern child-rearing literature asserts that parents can do irreparable harm to the children's social and emotional development, modern parents must examine their words and actions for a significance that parents in the past had never imagined. Besides, psychological experts disagree among themselves. Not only have they been divided into competing schools, but they also have repeatedly shifted their emphasis from one developmental goal to another, from one technique to another." [1]

When being interviewed on CBS morning news in December 1978, about a book he had recently written concerning child development, an eminent child psychologist made some interesting observations. Asked if we could rely upon his new findings in view of the fact we had mistakenly followed another view in raising our children for twenty years, the psychologist replied with uncommon honesty, "Developmental psychology, as a science, is too immature to accept any statement as infallible." These views, however, overlook the fact that there are some moral and spiritual absolutes. Psychological technique and theory may shift, but Bible-based principles never change.

Rebellion is not always apparent even to the most perceptive parent. However, there are generally some signs that will help determine if your child has a problem.

Here are some guidelines to help you in evaluating your special child:

1. Has there been a prolonged (more than a week or two) period of change in usual eating or sleeping habits?
2. Is there a definite change of at least the above length in personality traits, i.e., a quiet child becoming suddenly talkative or a pleasant child acting worried or morose?
3. Is there a change in school performance, either socially or academically?
4. Is there a drastic change in appearance, either from neat to sloppy or vice versa?
5. Is there a not-so-easily-defined, but strongly-felt difference in any other way? Many parents have an intuitive awareness that something is not right.
6. Are there observable evidences of antisocial behavior, i.e., lying, stealing, cheating?

If two or more answers to the above are yes, it is wise for the parents to confer with each another and perhaps another trusted adult such as a teacher, pastor, relative, or youth counselor. If each agrees on observing these problems, it is time for a conference with the child. Usually, such a troubled child will leave notes, poems, or articles hinting at serious problems. These notes, often left purposely for the parent to find, are sometimes silent cries for help. It is not being invasive, but wisely protective, to read them and even quietly look for other evidence of drug or alcohol usage.

In evaluating the existence or severity of a problem, common sense and instinct are invaluable. People were raising children successfully long before developmental psychology was established as a legitimate academic discipline. It is a serious error to let the experts make all the decisions about rearing your child. Love and a lot of good judgement are often superior to psychological technique. The pressure of modern society, however, has encouraged some serious errors in the home. These errors should be examined, but no parent should lose his self-confidence about raising his children. The overzealous approach to conscientiously do everything just right, to measure each word and response, may create problems.

Some of the more common causes of child rebellion in the home are worthy of consideration.

Natural Personality Differences Between Parent and Child

Differences in personality or temperament of children are not fully understood by modern researchers, although an awareness of the phenomena dates all the way back to Hippocrates. There is continuing debate on whether these differences are genetic or environmental. Temperamental differences can create serious problems between parent and child if the parent fails to recognize, understand, and respond to the problem.

When a placid mother has an active child, the parent can suffer extreme frustration. The quiet and generally calm mother may find the normally active child's behavior very irritating. In an effort to deal with the problem, she may try to restrict the child's activities for her own peace of mind. In the process of trying to force the child into her own emotional mold, she may harm the child's natural personality development. Care should be used to distinguish between natural personality traits and deliberate misbehavior.

In contrast, an active mother may believe her quiet child is abnormal. Her perception and expectations of the child can create early conflict and unnatural pressure for the child to change his behavior. The mother may unknowingly communicate to the child her disapproval and unhappiness. Negative conversation about him in the presence of the child may lead to a poor self-image and the onset of an early cleavage between parent and child.

Parents with poor self-images may also see their own personality traits in their children and find them distressing. Out of distaste for himself, a parent may try to pressure a child into a mold he cannot fit. Dissatisfaction with one's self may be misdirected toward a child with disastrous consequences.

Parents may also see in their children personality traits they find distasteful in their marriage partner. The rise of divorce and unusual stress in the home has heightened this problem. The parent who has tolerated the trait in a marriage partner may make an unrealistic, but determined, commitment to reshape the child. The effort may strain the marriage relationship as well as damage the child's natural growth. If a child persistently hears in response to behavior disapproved by his mother, "He is just like his father," the child will eventually learn that both he and his father are undesirable. That message, carved into his brain by repetition, can set off a multitude of unhealthy behaviors and internal feelings about himself.

② Disappointment in a Child

A father sat watching 125 third- and fourth-grade children practicing flag football at the YMCA practice field. There were five or six teams scrimmaging simultaneously. His eight-year-old son was developing his skills as a linebacker.

Next to him there was an animated conversation in progress between two approving fathers. On that practice field there were 124 boys and one girl. The little girl, like the rest, was fully attired in football shoes, oversized helmet, jersey, and appropriate football pants. Her father was explaining to his companion how hard she could block and how well she could tackle. This whole exercise, he observed, with a condescending smile, was really too tame for her because she was accustomed to playing tackle football.

The eavesdropper listened further as the little girl's father explained how only the week before he had raised her basketball goal to regulation height because it was no longer a challenge. He humbly admitted that his college experience at these sports had helped her considerably. Alternately, he yelled encouragement to his daughter and moaned at the ineptitude of her competition.

The observing father felt certain that he knew what was happening, but could not resist inquiring. He purposely asked only one question, "How many sons do you have?" A cloud abruptly brought an end to all the excited conversation, when the man responded that he had no sons, only two daughters. This father was obviously disappointed that he had no sons through whom he could vicariously live out his fantasies of catching passes for the Dallas Cowboys. One day, and perhaps very soon, that little girl would discover that her father is unhappy about her being a girl. The recognition of that disappointment will inevitably affect her view of herself and her relationship with her father. The father's involvement with his daughter was self-centered, not child-centered.

Disappointments in children take many forms, all of which, when perceived by the child, are painful. They may, if serious enough, create despair or alienation and a sense of rejection. An article in a recent periodical illustrates this point.

The phone rang in a fashionable suburban home. "Hi, Mom, I'm coming home."

A serviceman in San Diego had just returned from active duty. His mother was wild with joy. Her boy was alive.

"I'm bringing a buddy with me," he said. "He got hurt pretty bad. Only has one eye, one arm, and one leg. He has no home, and I'd like him to live with us."

"Sure, son," the mother said. "He can stay with us for a while."

"Mom, you don't understand. I want him to live with us always."

"Well, okay," the mother relented. "We'll try him a whole year."

"But, Mom, I want him to be with us always. He's in bad shape . . . one eye, one arm, one leg."

The mother became impatient. "Son, you're too emotional about this. You've been in a war. The boy will be a drag on you."

Suddenly the boy hung up.

The next day the parents received a telegram from the Navy. Their son had leaped to his death from the twelfth floor of a San Diego hotel.

When the boy's body was shipped home the parents found he had one eye, one arm, and one leg.[2]

A midwestern family named Blue, motivated by deep concern, began to assist battered children by keeping them in their home. Each child was placed by a reputable county agency. Over a period of three years several very young children had stayed in their home for brief periods of time.

A nine-year-old girl named April came to their home for an extended stay. April's natural father had been gone from her home for many years. Her brothers and sisters had been given up for adoption by her mother. On several occasions, April's mother had told her she did not love her or want her in her home. For brief periods of time the mother would turn the care of the child over to the county, but would soon demand that she be returned.

Whenever April would be staying in a foster home, her mother would call and continually disrupt the child's life, alternately vowing her love or renouncing the child completely. The child had been both orally and physically abused until she showed very obvious signs of stress.

One night when she was in their foster home, Mr. Blue heard April talking in an upstairs bedroom. Out of concern, not curiosity, he moved closer to the partially opened door to check on the girl. She sat in the middle of the floor with a rag doll in her arms, softly speaking to the doll just as though it were her child. She said repeatedly, "April, I do love you. I really do. You know I love you, April."

The little girl was feeling deep rejection and was trying to reassure herself she was really wanted and loved. Most children cannot bear rejection without permanent scars.

Some parents are disappointed with a child's appearance. That disappointment is not necessarily related to physical deformities. Frequently, a child born with a serious physical handicap will be the object of even more intense attention and love than normal children. A child may have the physical features of some relative or a mate whose personality and behavior are distasteful. "He looks just like his Uncle Harry," and the fact that the uncle spent ten years in the penitentiary may make both parent and child uncomfortable.

Parents are occasionally disappointed in a child's intellectual skills. Parents with above-average intelligence may feel and communicate disappointment toward a child who is not intellectually inclined. The parent, who unfortunately feels the child is an extension of himself, takes the child's deficiency as a reflection against his person. Few children fail to sense that parental disapproval. Severe damage can be done to the child who comes to believe he is a failure in the eyes of his parents. Again, the self-centered approach to child rearing is damaging. The sooner a parent accepts the fact his child may not fit his ambitions for him, the better it is both for parent and child.

Parents are sometimes disappointed in a child's vocational interests. Traditionally, parents want their children to enter a job or profession that is equal or superior to their view or society's view of a "good job." The child's values may very well be superior to the parent's. Having watched a father injure his health, leave the family for extended periods of time, and suffer continual exhaustion, a child may decide he wants a simpler life. Although the father may be unhappy with his son's choice, the child may live a far more satisfying life. In recent years the pressures of upward vocational mobility have encouraged many children to reject the ideals of their parents.

Continued expression of disappointment in a child because of his behavior may drive a child to even worse activities. Tell a child that he is a "bad boy" long enough, and he will become one. In fact, a parent's perception of his child may become a self-fulfilling prophecy.

A group of researchers in a California school administered IQ tests to elementary children. When the tests were completed a number of students were selected at random. The teacher was informed that the tests revealed these pupils to be on the threshold of significant intellectual development. At the end of the school year, tests were administered again. It is interesting to note that those children who were randomly selected scored a significant improvement in IQ above the balance of the students who were tested. The only variable was the teacher's view of the child. Believing the child was capable of further development, she made it happen without even knowing it.

Your expectations of your child can affect what he becomes. Disappointment, when perceived by the child, can be a devastating blow to his positive development. Expect and develop spiritual qualities in a child as well as social and mental ones. There are a multitude of Bible promises upon which you can rely. You cannot change the physical appearance, the sex, the athletic ability, or the native intelligence, but you can positively encourage his spiritual growth. "Train up a child in the way he should go: and when he is old, he will not depart from it" (Proverbs 22:6).

Use discretion when you express praise to a child. It can have a negative impact if you continually express approval of the wrong things about a child. If you continually tell a girl that she is physically attractive, you may be certain that in her response to the need for approval, she will be preoccupied with appearance. She may, in fact, neglect more important spiritual and personal qualities because of your failure to encourage them.

Praise is a vital part of the developing self-image of a child. It must be given specifically, honestly, and at the right time.

A grandmother was overheard in conversation with her nine-year-old granddaughter. She sat facing the child for a while, looking her directly in the eye. She said, "Michelle, I want to tell you something very special. I saw you at school yesterday talking with your teacher. You were looking him straight in the eye, and you spoke so clearly and honestly. You did not act the least bit shy or afraid. I want you to know I was very proud of you." That child is likely to relate with other adults and with similar candor.

Never attack a child's person when you discipline him. Although not intended, a parent may imply disappointment in the child rather than his behavior. Some years ago a nineteen-year-old youth came to a pastor for counseling about the communication gap between his father and himself. At the early age of ten, his father often sent him to the tool box for a wrench. The boy confided that his stomach would knot up while he frantically searched, knowing that each moment he delayed his father was becoming increasingly angry. When he failed to find the tool, his father would call him "stupid" and then get the wrench himself. The boy had grown to believe he *was* stupid, and to this very day when asked to get a tool for his father, the knots return to his stomach.

You may not be able to see it, but your child wants and needs your approval. When he fails to get it, he may resort to desperate ends. Attempts at suicide are frequent tools. The most painful battle a child ever fights is to maintain the approval of his parents while in conflict with their values.

Misguided Expectations

Every caring parent has goals for his children. There is a point at which those behavioral goals may come in conflict with the realities of possible achievement levels and the well-being of the child. Every parent needs to evaluate what he expects from his child. When do the expectations for your child's behavior become detrimental to his development? One guideline that parents might consistently apply is a simple question that provides perspective: "Is my child's current behavior going to be important when he is twenty-one?"

A mistake commonly made by new pilots is to overcontrol an airplane. Normally, only minor course corrections need to be made. Overcontrol is uncomfortable for passengers and unnecessary for positive navigation. Overzealous parents may be guilty of the same error with their children. Frequently, minor course corrections are more effective when you have in view the whole journey of a child's life.

Parents should have realistic expectations of their children. Expectations about a child's behavior should consider his age. Children can be taught at a very early age to stay away from breakable objects left on tables. However, preoccupation with early potty training can be frustrating for the parent and nerve-racking for the child. A seasoned physician, consulted about a child who wet the bed, responded with the calm overview of experience that he had "observed children learn all through their young years" and added, "I never met a college freshman who wet the bed." Young children drop food at the table and often tip over glasses. It is quite normal, and both you and the child will survive, unless of course, you make it a matter of life and death.

Young children are not going to sit through an hour-long church service with the same attention as an adult. A child's attention span is shorter, and sermons are generally designed for adults. Young children will not sit still in a physician's office or anywhere for long periods of time, without moving and without something to occupy them. It is unreasonable to expect it.

The interests of children, including their reading habits, peer relationships, sense of responsibility, and intellectual growth, are related to age. Pushing children to learn or behave beyond the limit of their age creates anxiety and frustration and often lays a foundation for a child to rebel. Parents who tend to view their children as extensions of their own identities and achievements are more prone to this excess.

Mothers and fathers should have similar expectations for their children. It is an unreasonable and unnecessary burden for children to face differing and conflicting demands from parents. Parents need to agree mutually as to what is expected of children in the areas of studies, schedules, chores, and standards of behavior. It is confusing and unfair for parents to send different messages to their children regarding their behavior.

When parents disagree, a child may learn bad character qualities. By manipulating the parent who expects the least, an early pattern of deception may be formed. A child may also develop some guilt in having to make choices he knows will displease one parent. It is thoughtless and selfish parents who refuse to establish unified expectations.

Misguided expectations often reveal the internalized fears of the parent. A bright and caring mother approached a counselor with questions about her son's lack of interest in athletics. The father in the home had played baseball in a semipro league while in his twenties. Their twelve-year-old son, however, while showing great promise as a musician, was totally disinterested in athletics. He had played one summer of Little League, but did so only because he was pushed. The distraught mother admitted minor conflict between her husband and herself over the approach that should be taken. She believed the boy should be forced to play Little League ball, while her more relaxed husband disagreed. She really wanted the support of the counselor.

The counselor believed that he detected some fear in the mother, so he probed with a delicate, but necessary, question. "Are you fearful that your son is not masculine enough?" When she confirmed his suspicion, he asked further, "Are you afraid of a tendency toward homosexuality?" She smiled painfully and admitted that was her problem. The counselor confirmed the judgement of her husband and told her to stop worrying. To press the boy beyond the scope of his personal interest would drive him away and compound his problem by making him feel inadequate and rejected. The mother expected the wrong things from the boy because of her own fears.

④ Discipline

Punishment or discipline? Never punish a child. Every parent should discipline his children and learn to distinguish it from punishment. The Bible says, "And, ye fathers, provoke not your children to wrath: but bring them up in the nurture [discipline] and admonition of the Lord" (Ephesians 6:4).

The distinction between punishment and discipline (chastening) is very real and may determine the outcome of your child. Discipline has as its purpose changing the behavior of a child, not paying him his due for misbehaving. There is no useful purpose served by spanking a child or depriving him of privileges unless it results in his learning to act differently in the future. In fact, punishment always has its focus on the past while discipline looks toward the future. Punishment brings satisfaction to the one who administers it, while discipline, springing out of concern, is painful to the responsible parent. Punishment is administered in anger and hostility whereas discipline arises out of love and caring. Punishment ultimately makes the child angry, but discipline prompts him to love you.

David, the King of Israel, punished Absalom, his son, and the results were disastrous. Absalom murdered his brother, Amnon, for raping Tamar, his sister. David punished Absalom by banishing him from Israel for three years. Joab, David's general, persuaded David to let Absalom return to his homeland, but the king, still angry, refused to see him for two more years.

Absalom burned down Joab's barley field to force a meeting with his father. Joab, after five long years of absence, arranged for Absalom to see the King. David wept, but down in the heart of Absalom there was anger and bitterness that had been growing for half a decade. Shortly, Absalom organized an army, portrayed himself as the friend of the downtrodden, and overthrew his father from his throne. Rather than dealing constructively with his son's wrong, David punished him. David lost both his throne and his son. One of the first mistakes, then, of dealing with the misbehavior of children is to punish rather than discipline.

Discipline, in the right measure, needs to be administered at an early age. Solomon wrote, "He that spareth his rod hateth his son: but he that loveth him chasteneth him betimes" (Proverbs 13:24). The word *betimes* literally means "early," i.e., begin discipline when a child is young. Using good judgement is a key to success. Parents need to find the balance between brutality and permissiveness. It does not take a baseball bat to teach a young child not to throw food at the table or touch a potentially dangerous object. A harmless twig will do.

Measured discipline should begin early, including an occasional swat on the backside, and continue in some form until the child reaches maturity. A parent cannot let a child go for years without discipline, then suddenly begin and expect a child to respond with cooperation. Parents often use better judgement in training a new puppy than they do with their children. Physical punishment is of limited value after children reach the age of reason. By the time a child reaches this age, his understanding of ideas should make the well-disciplined child respond to reason rather than force. If a child requires force at age fifteen, you have failed to mold his mind. When a child is as strong as you are physically, all of your resources are gone if that is your only tool.

Discipline needs to be administered progressively. The moral laws of God are absolute. Underlying the universal legal codes of men are the Ten Commandments. It is always wrong to lie, to steal, and to murder.

The process of discipline, however, involves more than morality. Discipline involves an organized approach to guiding and structuring a child's entire life. This system includes the child's physical, spiritual, mental, emotional, and social well-being.

It is helpful if a parent understands the beginning and progression of discipline. In the first years of a child's life, the rules and regulations are intended for his physical protection, his emotional direction, and his social development. The very young child does not grasp abstractions, hence the moral concepts can only be understood later on. A parent needs to distinguish between rules that involve morality and those that are simply to protect the child during a phase of his growth.

Early in life a mother must teach her child to recognize and avoid dangers such as aspirin and bleach bottles, the hot stove, and the busy street. Parents then need to teach children to control and meet their physical needs, appropriately. Standards of interpersonal behavior need to be developed. These instructions will teach a child where to play, when to speak, how to eat, and reasonable schedules and limits.

As the child develops, the nature and amount of discipline change. Instruction becomes progressively less detailed and more abstract. The blueprint is being transformed into the structure of the child's world, and he is taking an increasingly active role in making choices. When wise decisions demonstrate a child's maturity, the parent needs to cautiously decrease his supervision. The child needs opportunity to make independent choices while the parent is still there to guide him when he needs help. The home is never an absolute democracy. The older children grow, however, the more they need to be involved in the establishment and understanding of policy.

Some time ago a girl came to a pastor for counseling. Both she and her parents were extremely upset over an incident in the home. An intelligent girl in her late teens, she had arrived home in the absence of her parents. She had an opportunity to visit with a foreign exchange student, a great interest of hers, just a few minutes from her home. She prepared a note explaining her absence and the time of her return, and placed it where she knew her parents would see it the moment they arrived home. She visited with the student, returned home at the time she had estimated, and was met with a storm of protest from her parents who insisted she had violated a rule about getting their prior consent. The girl was angry at her parents' reaction, and the incident escalated into a major problem in the home.

These parents overlooked the whole purpose of either rules or policy. The parents insisted they wanted to insure the safety of the child and to teach responsibility by their requirement of consent to visit a friend. The parents readily admitted that she was in no danger and that she had done what was outlined in her note. The spirit of their limitations had not been violated; rather, it was the letter of the law. This girl had been treated like a small child and not like the young adult she was. The girl was genuinely bewildered by the whole affair and so was the pastor. Where possible, policy rather than rules ought to prevail. Rules, without any reasonable foundation, create rebellion.

The purpose of discipline and guidelines is to teach responsibility to the child. Rules often teach only conformity. A child may conform without being responsible. Policy rather than a rigid set of inviolate rules gives the opportunity to learn from choices and evaluation of situations. William Glasser said, "Given an opportunity to learn this from kindergarten onward, children can become responsible and socially aware; we will then need fewer rules and punishments." [3]

Discipline needs to be administered without destructive anger. In the process of interviewing young people for this book, the following question was asked: "If you could change one thing about your father, what would it be?" The most common answer was that the father would not become so angry.

Uncontrolled anger without fairness is not an effective instrument for disciplining children. It generally provokes two unproductive emotions—fear and loss of respect. Anger provokes anger. Anger in the parent is often an outlet for his frustration. It is parent-centered, not child-centered. Habitual anger does not reflect love and caring, but it reflects selfishness and a lack of genuine concern for the child. The angry parent often reminds the offending child of the great sacrifices that have been made for his benefit, adding guilt to his fear, anger, and loss of respect. You may be certain that children are unmoved by these irrational reminders.

Unhealthy, destructive anger often arises out of uncertainty and fear. Such behavior is usually impulsive and is the expression of old habits, learned in childhood from one's own parent. When a parent is not sure he can gain the obedience of a child, he may explode. This may be a habit that he learned early in life to get his own way. Many parents have not realized that real strength can be expressed with a gentle firmness that is truly effective.

On the other hand, a person with controlled anger, or righteous indignation, knows what needs to be done and is willing to expend the energy to accomplish just that. This sort of anger does not instill fear, but confidence—especially in a confused and rebellious child who intuitively knows he needs external controls.

A counselor was dealing with a teenage girl who had learned to live by bullying nearly everyone around her. Most of her peers—and even adults in her life—were afraid of her explosive temper. On one occasion she pushed her counselor a bit too far. The usually even-tempered woman decided the time had come to deal with Cindy. She chose to express her own anger in a nicely controlled way—firmly, but with fairness. Cindy knew she deserved it: she became quiet and left the office. The next day she returned to her counselor's office and with unusual sincerity said, "I'm really glad you got angry at me yesterday. I had it coming! I never knew you really cared about me before!"

Never discipline a child in the heat of anger. If you have developed a habit of exploding in fits of temper at the misdeeds of your children, break it. Wait until you have cooled down before dealing with the problem. Both you and your child will be glad you did. Every time you deal with a problem in anger, you are driving a deeper wedge between you and your child.

Violent anger directed toward young children promotes secrecy and patterns of deception in them to avoid their having to endure the wrath of a parent. Many fathers, as well as mothers, are totally unaware that their children are deeply afraid of them.

As the years go by, the child is likely to get enough courage to deal with the problems just like his parent—in open anger. Then communication will steadily deteriorate between the two and they cannot discuss problems rationally. A pattern of blame emerges on both sides. The silence in a child often is internalized anger. The final result will be open rebellion when the child feels enough physical or emotional strength to fight or run away. In any event, when anger is carried far enough it will cause the parent to lose the child.

A teenage boy had been brought by his parents to a clinic for help. His anger and his behavior were uncontrollable. While in the clinic he wrote the following account of his thoughts.

I feel like I'm floating in space. Nothing around, nothing inside of my body except anger. Anger all over the place. Like if a bomb was ready to explode any second. Also, I feel that there is nothing at home. That with everything I do, I am going to get in some sort of trouble. That something else is going to be taken out of my room. Pretty soon, it seems as though I'm going to be sitting in a room staring at four walls in an empty shell. Also, it seems as though everything I say is a lie to them. No one believes me, no one cares what I think. That is one of the reasons why I can't talk to my father. Right now I think that I am living by myself. That no one is even aware that I live in the same house as they do. So I just [ignore] what they say. The only time, or the only thing I hear from them, is when I get in trouble or how my brother did in his basketball game. Or what my dad did on his business trip. So the way I feel is—forget them. Do what I want to do.

Also another thing. I have started smoking grass again heavily, and since I figure you are going to ask me why, the reason is, that it is just about the only time I have any fun. Especially when I'm really stoned.

The one thing that I would like to change is my feelings toward myself. The reason why for this is that I am unhappy at one time, then angry at another. Just like you have been talking about, most people can tell this. My teachers can, and also some of my best friends can. I try to hide, but every time I turn around, I'm back to showing it. Like I said, I have tried doing things to keep it out of my mind, but it doesn't work. There is one other solution I've tried and that is being stoned all the time. It doesn't help though. It just makes my dad mad when I come home hardly able to walk. So I am trying to be nice, easy, cool and collected. Really that isn't a solution, but it's really that hard to think up one.

Exercise discipline with warmth and love. The process of discipline includes correction, learning, and restoration, and normally results in warmth and love. Each time a child is disciplined, take him to a private room to avoid both interference and unnecessary embarrassment. Ask the child to explain the purpose and necessity of discipline. Any misstatement or misunderstanding should be corrected orally. Only after these steps, should the child be appropriately disciplined. A young child may require a spanking for a repeated offense, or an older child may be deprived of privileges. The child should be asked to explain why the action was necessary and encouraged to ask questions to resolve any misunderstanding or feeling of unfair action. Then comes the pleasant part, restoration. Open your arms and love the child as long as the child wants to remain. That love completes the cycle and relieves the child of the sense of rejection.

Inconsistent discipline creates confusion and alienation in children. It also creates a climate for the development of manipulative habits. Children need the emotional security and strength of predictable parental response and relationships. Clear, unmistakable guidelines need to be laid down for children to follow. The consequences of failure to comply should be just as clear and easily understood. Before it is administered, parents should make certain children understand perfectly the need for discipline in correcting misbehavior.

Correction in many homes depends totally on the mental attitude of the parent at the time of the offense, not on established guidelines for behavior. Drunkenness may compound the attitudinal problem because it tends to make the parent's actions irrational in the mind of the child. The child may escape correction for misbehavior if the parent is in a good mood. On other occasions, a bad day at the office may produce a violent beating for the same offense.

Children usually have a great sense of fairness. They know, early in life, when they have done wrong and experience an unpleasant sense of guilt about it. They crave absolution for this guilt and firm, even angry, punishment provides this. By contrast, if the child does not honestly understand his error, a punishment may damage him.

Young children particularly are damaged by inconsistent and patternless discipline. They may develop secret fears that carry over into other areas of their lives. They sometimes consider these apparently meaningless spankings or beatings as attacks on their personal identities. They develop a sense of personal worthlessness because they are disciplined without perceiving any pattern that relates to their behavior. As they grow older they may develop habits of dishonesty or feigned callousness to protect themselves.

Less intense forms of inconsistent discipline simply confuse children both about right and wrong and parental expectations. Loss of respect and eventual alienation are probable. It should be remembered, at the same time, that consistency alone is not the key to discipline; it is consistent and wise discipline. Some children maintain that dad is always the same, "always angry."

 Permissiveness

Dr. Benjamin Spock has been blamed at one time or another for almost all of America's problems, from the student revolution of the sixties to the fall of Vietnam. Now it is true that a generation ago he counseled young parents not to be so restrictive with their children; to respond more naturally to the child's needs. His famous book which sold over twenty-two million copies, *Baby and Child Care,* was published during an era of rigid rules of child care. Mothers were being told to wake their new babies every four hours for feeding whether they wanted to be fed or not. Spock, however, is not the chief culprit who led to today's permissiveness. It is a part of a much wider social problem related to the home.

It is true that there are some parents who spoil, pamper, and overprotect their children with the belief they are showing love, but instead raise incorrigible and irresponsible children. Some of them may have carried Spock's advice to extremes he never intended. In this generation, however, they are most certainly in the minority. Our problem today is far more serious and widespread than the doting parent of the past.

Permissiveness is neglect. Permissiveness among modern parents, in general, is not in response to the advice of Dr. Spock, but rather springs from neglect or indifference. Many modern parents, caught up in their own vocations and life goals, have found the care of children to be inconvenient. There is an observable trend to have fewer children, and many couples have decided to have no children because of the intrusion into their private lives. A recent survey of parents in their fifties indicated that a substantial number would not have children if they could do it over. Sociologists have called the new young-adult society of the seventies the "Me-centered generation."

Permissiveness today is often the failure to get involved in the life of the child—to take the easy way out. The child perceives this lack of discipline as lack of concern and love, and the result is predictable. Solomon wrote, "The rod and reproof give wisdom: but a child left to himself bringeth his mother to shame" (Proverbs 29: 15).

Often parents say, "I only want peace and harmony in my home. I want peace at any price." Generally what their actions show is that they are unwilling to set limits and enforce them if these go against the wishes of their child. They cannot tolerate the anger or disappointment this generates. They pay a high price for the questionable peace so attained. That price is the loss of that child through rebellion.

A child, in order to develop healthy emotional strength or identity, requires love and recognition of his self-worth. William Glasser maintains that identity is one of the single basic needs of every person: "[It is] the belief that we are someone in distinction to others, and that the someone is important and worthwhile. Then love and self-worth may be considered and the two pathways that mankind has discovered lead to a successful identity. If, however, a child fails to develop identity through love and self-worth, he attempts to do so through two other pathways, delinquency and withdrawal." [4]

Permissiveness by the parent is not an act of love, but neglect. It does not produce strong, creative, and emotionally healthy children. Children need limits, and they are a requirement for emotional growth. Limits imply concern for the child's well-being. When parents fail to set limits, children will continue to test until they meet with resistance. An observer of the Kent State riots noted the young people continued to surge toward the National Guard troops, testing how far they could go. "It was almost as though they were searching for the limits."

Rebellion is passive. Today, there is a new passive, nonmotivated rebellion. It is a social phenomenon seen chiefly, but not exclusively, in the homes of higher socioeconomic families. The father and mother are generally aggressive and highly motivated people. They have led busy lives and not being very involved with their children have set few limits. Their children have rarely, if ever, been able to please these parents who had unrealistic goals for them. At some point they simply gave up. These children, objects of neglect and disapproval, become passive and unmotivated. They gain attention from their parents by quietly rejecting their values. They are disinterested in grades, education, vocations, or life goals. It is an effective tool to force the attention of the permissive parent to the child.

Conflict Between Parents in the Home

Conflict in the home is not new. In the Bible it dates back to Isaac and Rebekah fighting over their twin sons, Jacob and Esau. Open conflict in the home, coincidentally with the working wife and liberated woman, is most certainly increasing. Children are the chief victims and suffer the most. It is the self-centered parent who allows serious conflict to errupt in the presence of vulnerable children. This does not mean that disagreements never arise in the Christian home. In fact, disputes talked out, with maturity and logic, can teach children how to resolve differences constructively.

Conflict in the home allows children to learn parent manipulation at an early age. Children will seize upon the opportunity to side with a parent in a conflict where they are most likely to get their way. They may in fact shift from side to side as they sense the emotional vulnerability of the parent who best serves their current aims.

A pastor counseled with a family for over a year in which the continual open conflict was a daily part of the lives of two preteen girls. The family was affluent and afforded more choices than usual, both in their activities and relationships. Frequently, the father would simpy not come home for days at a time. He would, without prior warning, fly from city to city in his private plane. From time to time he would call home and talk with his wife for long periods of time while she wept in the presence of the girls. He would then talk to the girls and promise them the fulfillment of every imaginable fantasy from expensive toys to personal meetings with teen singing idols.

The girls caught on quickly. They could go with dad for brief, frantic periods of time, and live in splendor. Mother soon felt she should compete with equally dazzling gifts and exhilarating experiences. The girls played both sides, while each parent set few limits for fear of losing the affection of the children. The children pitted the competing parents against each other so that their every whim was met.

Now, in their teen years, the girls have shifted their manipulative experience and demands to their peers. They do not understand why they fail to respond like mom and dad. They compete for attention, give and expect expensive gifts, spend money wildly, and are totally unaware they are the objects of ridicule. They have unwittingly been trained that they are at the epicenter of the world's attention and activities. When that fails to materialize in the more real world, they fantasize and weave amazing tales of fame and fortune to their unbelieving and embarrassed friends. These children will have extreme problems ever adjusting to the real world.

There are also deep spiritual implications when children are allowed to manipulate their parents. A child will often relate to God as he has to his parents. Children who have been allowed to manipulate parents sometimes see God as the great Santa Claus or Easter Bunny in the sky who is there for the sole purpose of meeting their every whim. When God does not respond as their parents, they sometimes turn away from Him believing He does not really care for them.

Conflict in the home may also cause children to feel deep guilt. Inevitably, conflict between parents involves the children. Parents often use children as tools in the battle with their mates much like children manipulate parents. One partner in a marriage may threaten to take the children from the other, or a spouse may be told that the children have no respect for him. Children, sensing that they are being used in a battle between parents, often develop a sense of guilt. The child somehow begins to believe he is responsible for the conflict, rather than being used as a weapon in the battle.

Conflict in the home generates deep fears in children. Aside from the fear of violence and confusion, there is a deep fear of divorce in almost all children. A pastor was in the ministry long before his wife became a Christian. During those years before her commitment to Christ, she deeply resented his involvement as a minister. The demands on his time were enormous and she, believing the congregation was her rival, complained bitterly. Frequently, during the grade-school years of their children, these arguments became violent, although the knowledge of them never went beyond the home. The wife continually harassed the minister and held over his head the threat of divorce, which would have put a swift end to his career.

The pain of those battles is vivid in the memory of one child, although over thirty years have passed. He lived in terror that his parents would get a divorce and that he would have to make a choice between two people whom he loved very much. So deep was his pain that he has a violent internal reaction when there is any disagreement between him and his wife in the presence of their children.

Parents tend to recycle their conflicts in their children. In the minister's home just described, there was a dramatic change at the conversion of the wife. In most cases, however, that does not occur and children learn from their parents how to battle with brothers and sisters in the home, as well as with mom and dad. A cycle or pattern of conflict, as a means of problem solving, is passed by example from one generation to another.

The story of Isaac and Rebekah is one of the most vivid examples in the Bible of recycling conflict. Isaac and Rebekah had conflict over each other's partiality to their twins, Jacob and Esau. Their sons, learning from their parents, competed with each other until Esau tried to murder Jacob for stealing his birthright. Jacob fled for his life and went to live and work with his Uncle Laban. He worked seven years for the right to marry Rachel, Laban's daughter. Laban deceived Jacob and gave him Rachel's uncomely sister Leah. Soon Jacob had married both sisters, who immediately began to fight with each other. Their battles continued for the next twenty years. The two sisters were competing for Jacob's love and attention. They gave Jacob twelve sons, each of whom bore a name for the rest of his life that would remind the child of the conflict in which his mother was involved.

The story of recycling conflict does not end with the two mothers. The brothers then fought among themselves. They took their brother Joseph, because they were jealous of his relationship with their father, and threw him into a pit with the intention of murder. Reuben, one of the brothers, intervened, and they then sold Joseph into slavery. Conflict is bad enough for two adults, but it is criminal to teach it to your children. Practiced anger will finally turn on the one who taught it.

7 Divorce in the Home

The United States has the highest divorce rate in the world. In 1978 there was one divorce for every two marriages. The rate has climbed dramatically since 1930 when divorce was rare.

Divorce is perhaps the greatest social tragedy because marriage failure damages so many lives. Divorce is traumatic for the two adults involved, but it is mind shattering for the children. The loss of a child's parent through divorce may have a more profound effect upon him than loss of one by death. At least in death the event is final, but in divorce its torturous memories and effects go on for years. Divorce is not a final rupture of a relationship like death, but a series of ruptured ties that are endless for the child.

Visitation rights are established by the courts, financial arrangements are imposed, and the child is shifted back and forth between parents for years. Summers with one and winters with the other, and all the while peer relationships and school schedules are disrupted. The whole affair usually has its focus upon the selfish desires of the parents, not the well-being of the child.

One of the cruel effects of divorce is that a child is forced to take sides. Inevitably, a child is hooked into the debate as divorce is contemplated. Competing parents often vie for the child's loyalty and affection prior to the legal division in the home. Often a judge may consult with the children themselves in bitter custody battles. This may not be a favor, since no child should have to decide between two parents. There has been a recent increase in divorce settlements where neither parent wanted the children. That must be the ultimate feeling of rejection for children.

The results of divorce are usually anger and despair. Most counselors will verify that children of divorced parents are uniformly angry with one or both parents over the separation.

A pastor sat interviewing an eighteen-year-old high-school senior in a basement office of a Christian school near Chicago. He asked if the boy had ever seriously considered suicide. The teen told a story of anger and despair. His father and mother had been divorced ten years before. His father had won custody, but he spent his summers with his mother. He despised his stepmother and blamed his father.

During the interview the boy told the pastor that only one month before their conversation he had gone to his bedroom, locked the door, and made preparation to take his life. He carefully loaded a .38-caliber revolver, placed the muzzle against his right temple, and pulled the trigger. The firing pin broke, and the gun did not discharge. His anger and frustration were so intense that he had preferred to die rather than be torn back and forth between father and mother. There are few children from divorced homes who are neither depressed nor rebellious. Children are not emotionally equipped to stand the strain of divorce, yet their interests are usually the last to be seriously considered.

Poor Communication in the Home

Over 90 percent of all children interviewed in search of the roots of "teenage rebellion" maintained that communication in the home was inadequate. Tragically, a majority of parents fail to sense the breakdown in communication or blame the failure exclusively on the child. It is clear from listening to one hundred young people that they take a totally different view of the matter. It is true that there has always been some separation between generations, but seldom in the history of man has the breakdown of communication between parent and child been so severe. What is there about these days that make them unique?

If a father is fifty years old, he was raised in a totally different world than his eighteen-year-old son. The father's frame of reference is quite unlike his son's and, although he may not recognize it, his own childhood was light-years away from that of his child.

First, there has been a knowledge explosion. The volume of man's knowledge is doubling every seven years. The child is in an educational system that is vastly advanced from that of his parents. Our college degrees have not prepared us to understand the math taught to our junior-high children.

There has been a social revolution. Peer relationships, with the move to suburbs, early mobility, and the introduction of television, have scrambled social ties and heightened social awareness. The civil-rights awakening is only twenty years old.

The son generally knows little about his father's work, and fathers know less and less about their children. Because of the breakdown of close family ties, teens tend to get more information from and develop closer ties to their peers than in the past.

There has been a moral revolution. The tolerance of immorality is a growing social phenomenon. Common among a long list of widely accepted practices are prostitution, illegitimate pregnancies of teenagers, cheating, stealing, dishonesty at all levels, rape, and premarital and extramarital promiscuity. The use of alcohol and marijuana is widespread, and abortion is considered an option for a majority of young people. The values of today's young people are totally different from their parents.

There has even been a language revolution. Our world is changing so rapidly that new words are added to the teen vocabulary daily, and there is a continuing shift in the meaning of words.

Straight Talk Gets Shafted

Remember when "hippie" meant big in the hips?
 And a "trip" involved travel in cars, planes, and ships?
When "fix" was a verb that meant mend or repair,
 And to be "in" meant simply existing somewhere?
When "neat" meant well-organized, tidy, and clean;
 And "grass" was ground cover, normally green?
When lights, not people, were switched on and off
 And the "pill" might have been what you took for your cough?
When "fuzz" was a substance that's fluffy, like lint,
 And "bread" came from bakeries, not from the mint?
When "roll" meant a bun, and "rock" was a stone,
 And "hang-up" was something you did to a phone?
When "swinger" was someone who swung in a swing,
 And "pad" was a soft, sort of cushiony thing?
Words once so sensible, sober, and serious are making
 the freak scene.
Like psychedelirious.
It's groovy, man, groovy! But, English it's not.
Methinks that the language has gone straight to pot!

American Flint

By the time this manuscript becomes a book, another group of words will undoubtedly replace these.

When a father tells a frustrated son, "I understand, I have been there," he is probably wrong. Their worlds are different, and it has greatly increased communication failure. The modern obsession of parents with careers, life goals, and television has further reduced conversation between parents and children.

Parents are listening to words, but the different frame of reference has cut off understanding. Parents must now listen with ears, eyes, and heart. Unless a child believes he is getting through, he will stop trying.

Pastor Dollar tells this anecdote:

When our youngest son was in kindergarten, he began to stutter. At first my wife and I, reluctant to discuss it, acted as if it would go away if we ignored it. It progressively got worse. One day—he was now in the first grade—he returned from school in tears. When questioned, he explained that the children at school were laughing at him because he stuttered. My wife and I were deeply moved by his obvious pain.

An inquiry was made at the school, and after he had been given a battery of tests by a speech therapist, my wife and I were invited to an evaluation session. We sat around a table about eighteen-inches high in chairs made for first graders. The therapist looked like a high-school student. She was very bright and well trained. The whole affair was very uncomfortable for me, however. I was accustomed to asking the questions, not answering them, but out of great concern for my son, I cooperated fully.

The therapist was aware that I was a minister, having seen our church services telecast. Her knowledge of my background as a public speaker prompted her to ask, "Is your entire family orally inclined?" I assured her that the conversation at our home was perpetual and animated. Knowing our son was the youngest child, she probed, "Could it be that he is trying to get the family's attention so he can break into the conversation? Could those efforts make him so nervous that he stutters?"

I really doubted that the answer to his problem could be so simple. I was already mentally making plans to take him to a clinic where equipment would be sophisticated, therapists better trained, and chairs designed for adults. The young therapist, not too comfortable herself, asked us if we would give her a chance to help our son. In fact, she asked if we would begin a simple exercise that very night.

Whenever our son began to speak, she advised we should all stop
talking, and look directly at him until he was through, making certain
that he was competing with no one while he spoke. We followed her
suggestion, and, to our utter amazement, he was much improved
before a week had elapsed. Before very long, the problem was con-
quered completely.

Children all over America are trying to speak to their parents, but
the competition is too great. Teens are weeping inside, and many are
angry because no one is listening. They become rebellious because
their words never get through. Your child has something to say to
you. It is important not because of his level of information, but
because of who he is and who you are to him. He is your child.
Listen—before despair sets in, and he stops trying to get through to
you.

 Double Messages in the Home

*The younger generation believes that American adults are hypo-
critical.* They teach one thing, but do another. Adults tell young
people not to smoke marijuana, but they drink alcohol. They tell
them that cigarettes cause cancer, but allow government price sup-
ports and let the industry continue to lure young smokers. Legis-
lators allow cigarette production even though there is convincing
evidence cigarettes cause lung cancer, but at the same time the FDA
tries to ban saccharin when there is limited evidence about its harmful effects. In 1979 the United States government will spend
seventy-five million dollars to subsidize the tobacco farmer, while
spending twenty-five million in a campaign to discourage cigarette
smoking. There must be observable adult integrity for children to
listen to their message. You cannot live by one standard and teach a
child another. The message does not get through.

Christian parents teach children that spiritual ideals and values are
the most important in life. They know, however, what we really
believe by the way in which we invest our lives. A parent who
spends most of his life making money at the sacrifice of his family

relationships will have a hard time teaching his child that materialism is wrong. The father who talks of honesty and integrity, but lies when the phone rings about his presence at home, or admittedly cheats on his income tax, will find these values hard to teach his children.

Pastor Dollar relates the following story about double messages:

> My oldest son had an automobile accident when he was sixteen years old. On a rainy night he failed to observe a stop sign and ran into the side of a new Pontiac. Over three thousand dollar's damage was done to the car he hit, and the collision was clearly my son's fault. A sympathetic but honest policeman cited him for failure to observe the stop sign, and he was summoned to appear in juvenile court.
>
> Before the date in court, I questioned my attorney about the need of representation. He expressed doubt about requiring it since my son planned to plead guilty and pay a fine. As a precaution, he sent a fledgling attorney to meet us just before my son was to appear before the judge. The young attorney, who formerly had worked in the juvenile court, spoke with us briefly in the waiting room, and, taking the citation, asked us to remain until he returned. In less than five minutes, he was out of the judge's chambers. He informed us the charge had been dropped. He then asked my son if he had any previous citations. My son, who had only had a driver's license two months, told him he had not. The attorney said, "Good. That's what I told the judge." The young attorney was gone without further conversation.
>
> I was speechless. I had tried to teach my children to obey the law. It seemed clear to me that my son would believe that I had arranged through my association with a powerful firm of attorneys to fix the ticket. I was angry and embarrassed. My values and the whole justice system needed some considerable explanation if my son were not to be damaged by the incident.
>
> We had a long lunch that day, and I apologized. I explained that it was possible to be guilty and not pay a fine, either because of who you were or whom you knew, but that it was wrong. I assured him that this was not an example of how I carried on our personal business affairs or those of the church I pastored. He listened and assured me that he understood, but I noted with dismay that he was still awed by what his

father had unwittingly arranged. It is also interesting to note that he has had more traffic fines between the ages of sixteen and nineteen than I have had in my entire twenty-five years of driving. I have sometimes wondered if there were a casual relationship.

The double bind is a bind. Another form of double messages is the "double bind." Teens request permission to participate in some activity, and the parent objects. The parent, by his answer, really punishes the child who makes the request. The message really comes through as, "Yes, you may go, but I will be angry if you do." That kind of permission is not in the child's best interest. If a parent really believes it is not good for the child to participate, the request should be denied and a reasonable explanation given. It serves no useful purpose to make a child feel discomfort or guilt when you give your permission.

Common causes of problems with teenagers:

1. Natural Personality differences
2. Disappointment in a child
3. Misguided expectations
4. Discipline
5. Permissiveness
6. Conflict between Parents in the home
7. Divorce in the home
8. Double messages in the home

Chapter 6

Why This Child?

How—or why—does it happen that in the same home one child is rebellious and the others are not? Let us consider this particular situation next.

President Jimmy Carter excelled academically at the United States Naval Academy at Annapolis, graduating in the top 10 percent of his class with a degree in engineering. After a distinguished career in the navy, he was elected governor of Georgia. He won the Democratic nomination in 1976 and was elected to the presidency. Carter is smooth, urbane, sophisticated, and at home with world leaders.

Then there is Billy, the president's brother, merchandiser of peanuts, hype, and influence. While serving in the military he spent thirty days in the brig and has been portrayed in the press for his misbehavior and his penchant for drinking beer. Billy seems to have an opinion about everything from foreign policy to the competence of the White House staff, and he is willing to share it all with eager reporters. He has probably been a source of embarrassment to his famous and dignified brother.

It is of interest to note that the brothers were both raised in the small town of Plains, Georgia, attended the same elementary and high schools, and were both disciplined by their strong-willed mother, Miss Lillian. The boys had—for the most part—equal opportunities economically, and, in general, they had the same home background. One became president while the other has been the object of serious criticism. Their sister, Ruth Carter Stapleton, a faith-healing, globe-trotting evangelist, was virtually unknown until her brother became president. She writes books and creates few problems except minor flaps over gaudy dresses worn in Moslem countries. Their other sister, Gloria Carter Spann, is the wife of a farmer who raises wheat and soybeans.

Lyndon Johnson had an alcoholic brother who lived in the White House all during the years he served as president. The brother jokingly referred to the home at 1600 Pennsylvania Avenue as his prison. Johnson was just more effective than Carter at controlling the antics of his brother.

In contrast, the Kennedy boys, John, Robert, and Ted, have all been achievers. One became president and each of them served with distinction in the United States Senate, with Ted still in office. All three have been the subjects of best-selling books. The limited information about their brother, Joe, who died in World War II, indicates that he came out of the same mold. The Kennedys have all done well in government and have been highly successful.

How can we explain the dramatic differences in children who come from the same family? One of the most frequent questions asked counselors is, "Why did this child rebel and the others did not?" It is not hard to explain when all of the children in one family turn out badly. What seems more perplexing is the development of rebellion in one child while his brothers and sisters mature without a serious problem. Upon closer examination, however, an explanation is possible. The belief that all the children from the same family should achieve, speak, and behave basically the same is based upon an erroneous presumption that familial influence is static. The truth is that every family is a dynamic system, continually in a state of change. No two children were ever raised by exactly the same set of parents because mothers and fathers are constantly in a state of change themselves.

Genetic factors which influence mental, physical, and emotional potential also vary within families. In the Kennedy family, one daughter, Rosemary, was born mentally retarded.

There are a variety of reasons why children within the same family may be quite different.

Physiological Differences

Only recently has there been any discussion of human cloning. At our current level of knowledge about genetics, there is great doubt that artificial genetic reproduction is possible. Even if it were successfully accomplished in one instance, it underscores the fact that the rest of the human race is genetically different. No two children are physically, mentally, or emotionally the same. One child in the same family may naturally be more sensitive to light, sound, or discipline than the others. Another child may be born mentally retarded, while a brother or sister in the same family is precocious. With all the discussion about cloning, test-tube babies, and genetic planning, each child is still unique.

Children are born with varying potential. Cousins of one of the authors had differing physical builds and abilities. One of the brothers was academically and athletically inclined. In college, he ran the one-hundred-yard dash in 9.3 seconds and maintained a high-grade-point average. The other was larger, slower, inept as an athlete, and a high-school dropout as a sophomore. His was, in contrast to his brother, a serious discipline problem, and he was socially maladjusted.

An undiscovered physical problem can disrupt a child's life and generate accompanying social and emotional problems. A boy in a suburban school of a large midwestern city had serious academic problems. He became a loser socially, as well, and was suspended from school on numerous occasions. He was continually in a battle both with school officials and his parents. The walls of his bedroom were punctured with gaping holes, where he had driven his fists in fits of anger and frustration.

His two older sisters and brother had been model students. The school system provided counseling but with little success. Psychiatric care was begun as the boy's academic and discipline problems worsened. It was after all of this disruption that doctors discovered he suffered from dyslexia, a sight dysfunction which makes letters on a page register exactly backward in the brain. The boy simply could not read because of a physical problem, but no one knew. By the time his physical difficulty had been diagnosed, he had developed a life pattern of hostility and rebellion.

Children are born with differing congenital temperaments. Admittedly, information is limited, but it is generally conceded that at least a part of the explanation is genetic. While it is believed that personality modification is possible, the changes that can be made are only moderate, especially after the fifth year of a child's life.

It should be clear that these differences in temperament frequently dictate the dynamics of parent-child relationships. The tensions generated by these differences, depending upon the wisdom of the parents, can either encourage or discourage a child's development. A child then, who is born with congenital physical or intellectual deficiences, may be prevented from reaching even his limited potential by the influence of the home. The natural physiological problem, in concert with the home environment, may cut off one child from developing at the same pace as the other children.

It is often parental response to natural differences that encourages even greater variation between children in one family. A child who has natural athletic ability may receive an unusual amount of attention and praise while a child in the same home who has musical talent is ignored. The child with musical abilities, having little athletic skill, may excel musically, competing in an effort to receive the attention of his parents. If his excellence in one area does not win his parents' attention, he may give up and rechannel his energies into misbehavior. The value system of the parents largely determines which child receives encouragement and which is ignored. Almost invariably the parents are unaware of their partiality to one child and the damage this causes.

A severely handicapped child often becomes the object of great love and attention in a home in compensation for the child's deficiency. Another perfectly normal child may be unwittingly neglected and in reaction become resentful. That hostility and anger can grow into serious rebellion. Parents with severely handicapped children should involve the other children in caring for the less fortunate one. Making the care a corporate effort will tend to strengthen family ties.

Special attention needs to be focused upon each child, not just the handicapped one.

Psychological Differences

Every child is unique physically, emotionally, and intellectually, but each requires the approval of his parents if he is to develop his potential. The goal of a home should not only be to accept a child as he is, but also to encourage his maximum development. All children should be loved and accepted for who they are and approved for their achievements. They are more likely to achieve if their best efforts are met with unqualified praise.

The first child in a home generally receives more attention than subsequent children. Childbearing under normal conditions is an exhilarating experience. Many fathers can recall the most insignificant details surrounding the first birth in a family. Later births tend to become a blur, and the emotions are not so deeply etched. The newness of the experience itself tends to focus more attention upon the first child.

It is likely that a first child will be noticeably different from other children in the family. Studies indicate that the first child is more likely to become an achiever than the other children. There is no indication whatsoever that first children are different physiologically. Any difference which may occur is widely believed to be attributable to the quality of parent-child relationships. There are a variety of chronological influences that affect children's development. The trend toward fewer children in each home has tended to bring greater focus upon the problems.

The eldest child has no competition for attention. The attention of parents, grandparents, and other relatives is focused exclusively upon him. His slightest cry may be cause for alarm and each new tooth cause for celebration. He receives unusual attention and stimulation. The closeness of the first child to the parent produces a stronger desire to please the parent. Hence, first children tend to grow into responsible, achieving adults more readily than subsequent children.

The first child is most likely to be overprotected until the birth of the second child. Feeding time must be precise, naps are scheduled, daily walks and playtime are systematic, and a sneeze prompts a frightened call to the "knowing" pediatrician. Fewer bruises and bumps and less exploration are allowed. The new parent must learn that minor cuts and bruise's heal, knots go away, and even broken bones mend. Most parents look back with some amazement at their reaction to the first child.

PARENTAL REACTION TO THE SECOND CHILD. The second child often suffers some neglect out of reaction against the parents' anxiety toward the first. Child rearing is a more relaxed process after the first child. Parents know what to expect, have fewer fears, and tend to take the experience in stride. By the time the third child is born, parents tend to reach a balance. It is axiomatic that middle children are more likely to create problems than a first or third child.

The fact that so-called middle children tend to create problems should never become an acceptable reason for misbehavior. If either you or your child is willing to excuse unacceptable social behavior because of his chronological order of birth, the pattern will be sealed for life. William Glasser makes a keen observation in his attack on Freud's practice of diagnosing mental illness. Glasser notes that once a patient has been told, "You are a schizophrenic," or "You are paranoid," he has a psychological crutch for the rest of his life. Every time he acts irrationally, the patient excuses himself with, "Oh, I can't help it. I am schizophrenic." [1] Don't ever tell a child his misdeeds are alright or let him excuse himself by saying, "Oh, I can't help it. You see, I am a middle child."

The second child is frequently the object of the "I won't make the same mistake twice" reactions. A parent observes what he believes to be a parenting error with the first child and proceeds to correct it in the second. There are several dangers to avoid. You may have improperly diagnosed the reason why your first child acts like he does. Your efforts at correction may then result in two mistakes rather than one. It is also a possibility that your change in approach may be confusing to your first child. He may interpret your reactions as favoritism or rejection of him.

The key is the avoidance of extremes. Neither overprotectiveness nor casual permissiveness is desirable. It is highly recommended that both parents attend prenatal instruction classes before the birth of the first child. Some of the fears and mystery is thus removed. A more informed parent tends to be a more balanced parent. Learn to enjoy the first child, but do not neglect the second. One family, after the birth of the first child, refused to let him attend church during his first eighteen months. The overzealous parents were fearful of bacterial contamination from some other child. Their child, while avoiding even a cold, failed to learn that he was not at the epicenter of all the world's activities. His behavior, to the dismay of nursery workers and friends of the family, clearly indicated he had missed that lesson. The child would have recovered fairly quickly from the normal childhood diseases, but he may never recover from egocentrism.

INCREASED PARENTAL MATURITY. "It's too late. I wish someone had told me these things twenty years ago." That statement or its equivalent has been heard at the conclusion of many lectures on child rearing. It does seem tragic that the insights at forty could not have been applied to children when parents were young. Remorse over learning, too late, some information about children is nonproductive.

It is clear, however, that some children in a family differ because parents benefit from experience as they grow older. They become more flexible, more responsible, and learn to discipline by design, not by coincidence. The result is better disciplined and better adjusted children. In one family with five children, the first four had serious problems. The last child, born to the parents in middle age, was in every way a delight. Increasing potential maturity, then, can produce differences in children.

THE INFLUENCE OF VOCATIONAL RESPONSIBILITIES ON THE CHILDREN. Most parents progress through stages of vocational responsibility as they grow older. Typically, the first job carries with it less responsibility and more labor. The younger years may require fewer hours on the job because the position carries with it no administrative or supervisory responsibilities. Responsibility normally increases with maturity and experience. The middle years are often the busiest as maturity provides vocational opportunities that are substantially broader. The very opposite may also be true. A young father may find he must work long hours at less pay to make ends meet financially.

Many younger employees find it necessary to travel regularly if upward vocational mobility continues. Years of travel and family transfers from city to city may finally result in a more stable existence with location in the home office of some large corporation.

Vocational moves may bring a sudden end to the positive influence of the extended family. No longer can the uprooted young mother call upon relatives for relief from her responsibility nor can children learn the security of caring relatives. The increased responsibility may change a gentle, patient mother into an irritable and depressed parent.

In any event, the level of commitment to job responsibility is a changing thing throughout the parent's life. The requirements of a job's time necessarily affect the time available for child rearing. The time shift may explain why one child rebels and another does not. It is generally true that the more time parents devote to interacting with their children, the better the relationship will be.

No vocational decisions should be made without careful consideration of their effect upon the family. No promotion is worth the life of a child.

Shifting Family Relationships

Family structure and relationships never remain static. They may become closer, more distant, or strained, but they are never the same as the years go by. Like the gears of a large machine, each change brings other corresponding changes with constant movement. The changes vary from slow and subtle to rapid and obvious shifts in relationships. Many variables influence these changes.

The growth and number of children bring change. Households must adjust both socially and economically to each new addition. Limited resources must be spread among more people, including space for privacy and money for individual needs. The same amount of parental attention must also be shared with more children. With each new child, there will be an inevitable shift in family relationships.

The energy level of parents changes. Older parents may develop physical problems which keep them from engaging in sports or other strenuous activities. With advancing age, a parent may have less energy to expend. Age combined with job pressures may result in the father sleeping on the couch every evening while children develop feelings of neglect and rejection. Serious illness may restructure an entire family when it involves the principal breadwinner in the home. Children may even be forced to take jobs to supplement income while the mother takes on major economic responsibility.

Ruth Carter Stapleton explained why her brother Billy is so different. "He was the last child," she observed, "and the whole family spoiled him rotten." The real key to his problems was the loss of his father at the age of fifteen. She described their closeness: "From the time he was a toddler, Daddy took Billy with him whenever he could. As soon as he was old enough to walk and talk, they became almost inseparable. It was a familiar sight to see the two walking hand in hand from our house down the red-dirt road through the orderly rows of pecan trees to the cotton and peanut fields. There was Daddy with his broad-brimmed straw hat shaped like a fedora, wearing bib overalls, and Billy dressed just like him. When they walked through the fields, Daddy inspected the cotton or peanut plants, and Billy, though not yet in school, was his apprentice." [2]

Mrs. Stapleton reflected upon Billy's reaction to the death of his father: "Daddy's death was the hardest of all on Billy. Day after day he came home from school to an empty house. Even when Mother was there, she seemed locked out of his life by her grief. In his own way, Billy's grief equaled hers, and most of it he bore alone. He couldn't go to Mother. There was no one else he could share his pain with except maybe Sybil." [3]

The loss of Billy's father was so profound that at the close of his wedding ceremony at the young age of seventeen, he took time to drive by his father's grave and leave his new wife's bouquet on the grave marker.

THE SHIFTING ROLE OF THE MOTHER. When the last child enters school, mother often becomes bored and may insist on taking a job outside the home, or she may enroll in a local college. The number of mothers working outside the home for reasons other than economic necessity has been steadily increasing. Both the mother's location and investment of energy change as responsibilities formerly hers are redistributed between husband and children. Children may not be prepared for these abrupt changes.

Grandparents may be forced because of ill health or the loss of a mate to become new family members. All the roles are rearranged. While the separation from grandparents in early life results in one kind of stress, the return of grandparents in later years brings other pressures.

Older children leave home for marriage, or college, or they move into an apartment away from the family. Shifts in responsibilities as well as financial resources accompany these moves. The dynamic relationships within the remaining family are altered.

In summary, the relationships within a family are in a continual state of change from the day of marriage until the death of both mother and father. Every child in a home is cared for by his parents under differing circumstances. The change in conditions may explain varying results.

CHANGING MARITAL RELATIONSHIPS. The relationship between husband and wife, even when it is close, goes through an evolutionary process. Hopefully, the older adults grow the more stable the relationship between husband and wife will become. Confidence, trust, and predictability should characterize aging couples. These qualities tend to provide secure role models for growing children. That, however, is no longer true in our society. Marital disruption has created some of the most traumatic pressures on children. Young children tend to be less able to cope with marital strain, separation, and divorce than almost any other problem. Even older children, when divorce occurs late in life, react with confusion and hurt. Their personal maturity will dictate how they respond to such a crisis.

EXTRAMARITAL AFFAIRS. Extramarital affairs, when discovered by children, tend to damage their lives. Older children who have already extablished their own values and identity tend to be less affected. Younger children, however, often interpret such affairs as personal threats to their world. The safety and continuity of the family is attacked, and younger children often feel unloved and abandoned despite all the oral assurances to the contrary.

Extramarital affairs normally reshape the offended mate's attitude toward the family. A wounded mother may turn to the children for emotional support or begin a systematic program to destroy the respect of children for their father. In any event, it is impossible for the children to remain unaffected.

MENOPAUSAL CHANGES. Marital relationships during menopause may change markedly. Such changes will affect children of all ages some way. Many women pass through the change of life with only minor symptoms while in others the entire personality is altered.

In the middle years, which is the menopausal era, women are faced with a period of great emotional and physical upheaval. Their children require significantly less care. Their husbands are often experiencing the most intense vocational pressures, and mothers face the imminent loss of children from the home. In their need for attention and a tangible focus for living, they may tend to use the physical symptoms as manipulative tools. This is usually an unconscious device. Many women are observably different in their behavior during this time. Children may be confused by this abrupt change in personality and react in silent withdrawal or angry rebellion. Women need adequate medical supervision, and they need encouragement from the whole family to reinforce self-worth and a sense of purpose. They need a new focus for the abundant energy that the immediate family no longer requires.

SEPARATION OR DIVORCE. Separation or divorce changes the whole world of a child, but it affects each child differently. Anger at the parent who has custody may result if the child blames him for the loss of the absent parent. Fear and despair may grip younger children who simply cannot grasp the reasons for the loss of one parent. They may also fear that they, too, may be excluded if they displease the remaining parent. Separation or divorce may drive one child to inward, silent emotion or another child to uncontrollable weeping. Each child needs an impartial listener to hear his reactions to the divorce and to comfort his grief.

There is no question that separation or divorce is inevitably damaging to children and leaves deep and lasting emotional scars. Jesus said in discouraging divorce, ". . . Moses because of the hardness of your hearts suffered you to put away your wives: but from the beginning it was not so" (Matthew 19:8).

Spiritual Transformation

PARENTAL TRANSFORMATION. The life-changing experience of the new birth rearranges lives and homes. Parents who have neglected—or even abused—children can become caring and sensitive when they enter a personal relationship with the Saviour. It is the most profound experience of life.

Tragically, older children may have missed the benefits of the godly life because the change took place later in life. Children, who have never heard mom and dad pray or who have not seen them involved in church, may feel threatened by this experience if they have not shared in the new birth. One couple in their mid-forties who had come to trust Christ had an older son who did not understand their experience of personal salvation. His father related the experience to the authors. The boy's relationship with the family began to change. Often he would go alone to his room for long periods of time. The father, sensing a problem, spoke with his son in privacy. He questioned the boy about his silence and their changing relationship. The young man confessed to his father that he felt left out of the family from the time he and his mother became Christians. The family's life-style and conversation were different, while his remained the same. He knew his parents were praying for his salvation, and he felt excluded from the inner circle. The younger children in the family were enjoying the benefits of born-again parents and had the new security of a Christ-centered home, while the older son felt threatened and confused.

Parents, caught up in the joy of the new-birth experience, should exercise care that their attitudes toward unbelieving children do not imply inferiority or rejection. While parents are anxious to share their new experience with those closest to them, they cannot force the same spiritual decision upon a reluctant child. That choice is the ultimate life decision and must be made personally by each child.

Care must be taken not to expect changes in the children to parallel those of the parents. Such a spiritual life-style can only result from an inner, personal change produced by the indwelling Holy Spirit.

TRANSFORMATION OF THE CHILD. A child may experience spiritual transformation without his parents' consent or understanding. A personal trust in Christ, strange as it may seem, may bring a cleavage between parent and child.

Many parents who could, in some degree, understand drug addiction and the runaway movement have been paradoxically confused by their child's spiritual rebirth. Attitudes of some parents suggest they even prefer drugs and rebellion because they can understand them. This phenomenon is not new. Nicodemus with all his wisdom, when speaking with Jesus, asked for further explanations of the new birth.

Peer Pressure

The fragmentation and deterioration of the twentieth-century home has made peer pressure one of the principal influences in the lives of teenagers. Peer pressure has always influenced adolescent development. The impact of modern society, however, has increased this pressure immeasurably. When interviewed, young people from both Christian and public schools said they believed peer pressure to be a greater influence than teachers upon their beliefs and behavior.[4] Stratified peer pressure exists in both Christian and public schools with equal force.

The significance of peer pressure cannot be overemphasized. It is rarely the cloak-and-dagger drug pusher who introduces a young person to his first drug experience. Almost invariably this is done by his best friend. Peer pressure does not have the impact on all children, nor is the response of all children the same. Those who have developed a strong sense of personal self-worth are not easily influenced by others. The depressed child who has had few successes and could be generally classified as a loser responds very quickly to peer pressure. In fact, the only sense of approval these children may experience is that of their friends.

Young people by their choices within any group soon become naturally arranged in social strata similar to a caste system. Students who excel academically tend to group with more serious-minded students. Their interests, study habits, and teacher relationships all contribute to this grouping process. They sense that they are achievers. Most plan to attend college, and have much more to lose by irresponsible behavior than their less studious classmates. This academic subculture exists in public high schools. As one serious student put it, "A good education is available in most schools, but you have to make a conscious choice to get it."

Mediocre and poor students also are attracted to each other. Not having attained recognition for excellence, they often get attention by disrupting classes, smoking pot, drinking on campus, bizarre hair-styles, or by wearing weird clothing. They are eager to conform with a group because it gives them identity, support, and approval.

Teachers and administrators unwittingly fall into informal alliances with students who excel. It is not uncommon in public schools for two clearly identifiable groups to exist—disruptive students and the achieving students with their ally, the administrator. The alliance between the academic establishment and the successful student is an understandable one because faculty and administrators find vocational gratification, as do parents, through the accomplishments of their students. Often deep antagonisms exist between the two peer groups. Two children from the same family may be identified with opposite groups, depending on their academic skills.

Male athletes, along with their admiring female counterparts, often form still another group. Some of these students alternately identify with academic subculture or the underachievers. Traditionally, they are called the jocks and their primary peer-pressure group is determined by their college plans. The student whose athletic ability is sufficiently good to provide him with recognition or even a scholarship will identify with the academic subculture. Athletic subcultures tend to disintegrate rapidly upon graduation, while academic groupings tend to extend into adult life.

ACCELERATED SOCIALIZATION. In recent years, children, at a remarkably early age, have acquired knowledge traditionally restricted to adults. Some children, by the age of seven, talk seriously of "boyfriend and girlfriend," homosexuality, and explicit sexual experiences. These infantile "love affairs" create unnecessary anxieties and fears of rejection when their experience does not parallel that of adult role models. The foundation is thus being laid for an unnaturally precocious social development.

Younger children in a family also experience accelerated socialization by following in the footsteps of older brothers and sisters. They have an entrée to older social activities through both the newly acquired early mobility and the contacts of the older children in the home. Older children who may happen to develop more slowly usually feel threatened by the more rapid development of younger brothers or sisters.

Not too many years ago parents were cautioned against overprotecting their children. There seems little need today for such warnings. Television, magazines, radio, and movies provide more explicit information than children can constructively absorb. Parents need to be exceptionally protective in this threatening world. Since it is impossible to be totally protected from such exposure, parents should be prepared to guide the child to understand the dangers.

UNFAIR COMPARISONS. The achieving student often creates problems for his less studious brothers and sisters. Inevitably, younger children are reminded of the brilliance of a brother or sister who preceded them. In the event that younger children are not as academically gifted, they are perpetually reminded of a standard they can never match. They may feel discouragement or jealousy.

Students with unusual athletic, artistic, or other special abilities create similar unfair comparisons. Such comparisons tend to aggravate identity problems which already exist. Every child should be measured only by his own unique potential. Efforts at forcing children from the same family to be equally productive in the same areas are unfair and damaging.

SIBLING RIVALRY.   Sibling rivalry may be intense and absurdly unwarranted. It should not be encouraged. Good-natured competition can be an excellent motivator, but extreme rivalry between children may be an effort to gain attention from parents. Rarely does it express honest dislike.

One child may learn that by working and cleaning in the kitchen she gets praise from her mother who places high value on such interests. Another child, not so inclined, may feel that she is a failure only because she has no interest in cooking. A wedge between mother and child can be driven if she favors one of the competing girls. The girl whose interest does not conform to her mother's will probably feels rejected. Her self-image may be damaged, because she believes she is not meeting the expectations of her mother.

Find an area of life where each child excels and express your pride in his achievement. Parents must look for areas of success, and encourage the child by approval and support. Without this input a cycle of failure may emerge, and a child may be headed for trouble. Eventually, a child may simply give up his effort to be noticed by you. When that occurs, some form of rebellion will emerge.

Chapter 7

The Father—More Than a Biological Necessity

An extreme patriarchal system that disenfranchised women prevailed in most cultures until the twentieth century. The father's word and authority were absolute, and women were often treated as chattels. That whole system is disappearing in most industrialized nations, and the proper worth of the woman is being increasingly acknowledged.

Reaction, however, has set in, and as is often the case the pendulum has swung to extremes in the women's liberation movement. The militant feminists now are insisting that five major institutions—love, marriage, family, heterosexual sex, and religion—must be destroyed to free women from oppression.[1] The absence and loss of visibility of male authority in the home are fast turning America into a matriarchal society. We are only now beginning to feel its impact. We need understanding and balance in the father-mother roles in the home if we are to produce well-adjusted children. The roles ascribed to fathers and mothers in Scripture do not imply superiority or inferiority, but rather define functions and structure. The God-ordained structure is for the nurture and protection of fathers, mothers, and children. The changing role of the father needs particular attention.

One hundred young people were asked the following question:

"What person in your life has exercised the greatest influence in determining your behavior and beliefs? The influence can be either for good or bad, and the person may or may not be a part of your immediate family." The quick response of the majority was "My father." In each instance where a child named someone other than his father as the principal influence in his life (unless the father was deceased), there were clear evidences that the teen had fairly serious personal problems.[2]

The role of the father in the American home has changed radically since World War II. Those changes, at least statistically, have been in direct proportion to the increase in teenage problems. There has been an enormous amount of criticism about the changing role of women and rebellious children. The birth of the women's liberation movement, the phenomenal increase in the number of working mothers, and the newly heightened female sexual aggression, have been cited as principal sources for most of our nation's home problems. With the intense focus upon the woman and her changing role, the man has almost gotten off scot-free in the discussion about child rebellion. That analysis is both unfair and untrue.

The Abdication of Fatherhood

The typical modern American male has abdicated his role as a father. It was not a conscious decision but rather a response to current social values and pressures. In any event, there has been a rejection of the traditional and spiritual roles of the father. The values of men have changed every bit as drastically as those of women. In fact, the value changes of both men and women are separate pieces of the same puzzle. A recent survey suggests a majority of men now want their wives to work.

The male vocation has become the highest life priority. Our society has placed enormous value on vocational success. A man's place in the community is determined by his job. The unconscious acceptance of this value system has driven men to sacrifice health, marriage, and their children to make good at the office. In a nameless society, men have fought for identity and function at the sacrifice of more important values. A study was recently made of a 1978 graduation class of a midwestern osteopathic college. In a class of 150, there was a total of thirty-eight divorces among the 110 married students during the short span of their four-year medical-school course. While there is a variety of factors influencing these marital failures, it seems likely that if nearly 35 percent divorced during school, the rate of failures would be even higher with the additional pressures of a new medical practice. A substantial number of these young men were apparently willing to sacrifice their marriage for their career. Admittedly, there may have been other influences that affected this high divorce rate.

ECONOMIC PRESSURE AND ABSENTEE FATHERS. Inflation with its economic effect upon homes has allowed fathers to rationalize their commitment to a job. Children raised in an affluent society have totally different attitudes toward money than their grandparents. Children of the depression were savers and prudent in the expenditure of money. Their children saved little and became the first "Credit Card Generation." It was reported in 1978 by a well-known economist that the families in an affluent midwestern city could not economically survive thirty days without income.

Children of the seventies are showing little responsibility financially. Their parents who fared relatively better are having small success in teaching children to use money wisely. That has created additional financial burdens on the home. Many fathers are victims of the unrestrained spending habits of both the mother and the children as well as their own impulsive buying. The frustrated father has often rationalized his long hours and his own extravagance by blaming the balance of the family for spending more than he could provide. The mother and children develop hostility toward the father for his absence and feel their spending is justified as compensation for having no father. A pattern of blame and hostility emerges. The gap between father and family widens while each feels deprived and excuses his actions.

Fathers may be tempted to use a series of damaging devices to relieve these inner pressures. Withdrawal, blame, and self-pity are common but solve no problems. Exploding anger on mother, child, or friends does not help and only produces a loss of respect by those who are involved. Reaching for comfort beyond the family through gambling, drinking, or extramarital affairs ends in disaster.

Finding workable solutions requires flexibility, sacrifice, and the cooperation of the entire family. A healthy balance between material provision for the family and the physical presence of the father is essential. The Bible declares, "But if any provide not for his own, and specially for those of his own house, he hath denied the faith, and is worse than an infidel" (1 Timothy 5:8). In contrast, the father who fails to spend time with his family deprives them of an equally important influence in their lives.

The needs as well as the wishes of the entire family must be considered in the father's search for this balance. A financial crisis or hardship may emerge if, because of a sudden change in values, a father measurably increases his time at home. His anxiety over the material needs of his family may cause him to be moody and create an unpleasant atmosphere in the home.

It is the father's motives in establishing his time and energy priorities that will determine the family's attitude. When, out of love, a father labors sacrificially for long hours to provide the real necessities of life, appreciation and warmth will likely be his reward. If, on the contrary, his long absences are known to be prompted by his desire to escape tension in family relationships, the demands of his household, or the satisfying of his own ego, inevitably children will be resentful and are likely to rebel.

The father's chief function in many modern American homes has been economic. The father is the breadwinner. He is neither needed nor wanted in many families for any other function.

In the last twenty years the rapid rise of the cults has paralleled the abdication of the male as a father. No significant studies have verified a cause-and-effect relationship. Psychiatrists are, however, aware that great numbers of young people, alienated from their fathers, have gravitated to charismatic cult leaders. At least temporarily these leaders meet a need.

Found on the body of Jim Jones, the leader of the mass suicide in the South American jungle at Guyana, was the following note written by one who accepted his death command:

Dad:

   I see no way out—I agree with your decision—I fear only that without you the world may not make it to communism. For my part—I am more than tired of this wretched, merciless planet and the hell it holds for so many masses of beautiful people—thank you for the only life I've known.

It is apparent from the books and newspaper accounts of Jim Jones, his People's Temple, and his twenty-five-thousand-acre mission in Guyana that he was father to many. It was common for his followers to call him Dad or Father. At least 912 people believed in him strongly enough to die. Jim Jones systematically destroyed family autonomy by injecting himself into the family's relationships and communication.

Tex Watson, confessed murderer of actress Sharon Tate, and a member of the Charles Manson gang, persistently referred to the Manson cult as "the family." Stories of the bizarre leader, Manson, suggest that to his followers he was father. Manson, himself, never knew his father and was transplanted almost twenty times in search of a home in which he could adjust. He made his own family, becoming the father he never had.

In January, 1979, NBC aired a special three-hour program, "The American Family: An Endangered Species." A series of family scenes were shown among which was a story of two lesbians raising children. One scene showed them reading the Bible and praying together. A noted psychologist was asked if that relationship were normal. He apologetically admitted that perhaps there was something unnatural about the arrangement, because, if it became the norm, it would endanger the continued existence of the human race. These untraditional families have emerged partially as a result of recent confusion over the father's significance in the family.

What Children Need From Their Father

1. **STRENGTH.** There is a poster seen in many shops today that says,
"Only in gentleness is there real strength; only in strength, can there
be gentleness." In our culture, with its confusion of sexual roles,
men commonly do not know who they are. They are usually taught
they must be strong and this is interpreted by many as "Be tough."
"Don't cry, don't show fear, and don't admit to confusion or indeci-
sion." The macho image, currently discussed and acted out, does
not necessarily reflect true strength. In fact, it may well be an attempt to project a toughness that such a man secretly fears does not
exist. Men learn early in life to negate most of their vulnerable
feelings. Dr. Ketterman recalls this incident:

> One evening when our son was three, I was showing him a new doll
> belonging to his older sister. His eyes grew big with delight in her
> movable eyes and soft brown hair. He started to take her in his little
> arms and hug her, when he abruptly threw the doll on the floor, began
> to cry, and sadly exclaimed, "Boys don't play with dolls!" I was hurt
> for his tears and angry with the unknown source of such misinforma-
> tion!"

Playing with dolls, in the context of a father role, can teach a boy
how to be a good parent. This need not threaten a boy's masculinity,
but can give him a pattern for tenderness that will later be expressed
to his wife and child. Boys may even enjoy cuddling a stuffed animal
at night without risking being a sissy. If a preadolescent boy, however, is still playing with dolls, it is a symptom of problems.

Real strength comes from healthy self-acceptance. A popular saying expresses it well, "God made me and God don't make no junk!"
In a search for humility many people have forgotten that God made
man in His image, and they have made of themselves "worms of the
dust." A father who has the courage to accept himself as the reflection of God Himself can revel in the beauty of this image because it
speaks of God's greatness. Theologically, it is understood that man
is a fallen being, but even in that state he is capable of incredible

intellectual and creative achievements. The redeemed man is capable of fellowship with God Himself. In Christ, we have all resources available to us. Let's live like it!

PROTECTION. Children are vulnerable and sensitive, hence they are easily hurt, and they feel those hurts deeply. They are also relatively helpless. They need a protector. Fathers often step aside and are gone when the child runs to them for strength. Fathers need to be there, not just physically, but for the child's emotional nurturing.

A treasured memory from Dr. Ketterman's childhood illustrates this.

> In the springtime, Kansas often had severe thunderstorms. There was little to break the force of the violent winds on those plains and the rain was blown in torrents onto the porch of our home. It would even run into the house at times. While my mother would go to the basement, in a logical search for safety from possible tornadoes, my father was calmly standing on the porch, sweeping off the water to keep the house dry. As a child I had a choice, to join my mother in the safe comfort of the basement or to stay with my father. My childish mind, however, saw no need for a choice. I was truly safe only by my father. He and his broom were all the protection I needed.

DISCIPLINE. Some years ago, the Mormons observed that they were losing young people from their beliefs. There was great concern among the leaders of this faith since they highly value the family. Two students at Brigham Young University studied the problem in an unpublished master's degree thesis. Their findings revealed that children were lost through the quality of the father's discipline. The principles they proposed are sound. In summary, they concluded there are basically four types of fathers: *neglectful*—low in love, low in discipline (he avoids his children and flees all responsibility); *permissive*—high in love, low in discipline (he actually fears his children, who lead him); *authoritarian*—low in love, high in discipline (he fights with his children and forces obedience); *authoritative*—high in love, high in discipline (he leads his children and fellowships with them). It is clear both from this study

and from Scripture that the authoritative father is the most successful. This study underscores Paul's admonition, "And, ye fathers,
provoke not your children to wrath: but bring them up in the nurture
and admonition of the Lord" (Ephesians 6:4).

Children generally spend more time with a mother than a father. It
is she who feeds, nurses to health, and supervises daily events. She
scolds and guides, sometimes nags, or even yells out her frustra-
tions. There seems to be a callous that forms on a child's eardrums
so that he no longer hears her scolding. It is good for mothers to deal
with disciplinary problems as they arise. The father, otherwise, becomes her whipping boy! The child needs a new voice, and it is
desirable for dads when they are at home to observe misbehavior
and deal with this appropriately. A father's masculine voice, physical strength, and the fresh approach of his methods, makes him
effective.

Discipline affords an exceptional opportunity to reflect a picture of
the Heavenly Father. As the representative of Christ in the home,
the father has the responsibility of establishing guidelines and secur-
ing the honest cooperation of the mother in a unified approach to
discipline. The methods and manner of good discipline have already
been outlined.

In Psalms 32:8, we read, "I will guide thee with mine eye." Children almost instinctively look into the eyes of their parents. It is only
in response to anger that they learn to look away. They will read
instantly the feeling inside the parent's heart. If that is firm determination, the child is likely to obey; if it is rage, he will cower in fear or
return the anger; if it is teasing and fun, he will play; if it is doubt, he
will choose. Fathers need, then, to be clear about their feelings and
make them identical with their words. They must be honest, because
the child will believe what he reads in the eyes of the father, not
what he hears! They must be firm and clear so the child will learn to
obey.

VALUE. Through their early relationship, children no doubt take for
granted that they are special to their mothers. Today it is not so
common that they feel secure with the father. Much of the time,

children must test out this significant quality in their relationship with their dads. "Does Dad really care about me?" "Am I important to him?" "How can I be sure?" These are questions most children feel and rarely ask orally. They may, however, act them out in various attention-getting behaviors.

Partly due to vocational demands, dad's opinions and values are not as familiar to the child as the mother's. Dads rarely talk about their values or beliefs with their children. In our survey, one hundred young people were asked this question, "Does your father personally communicate to you his moral and spiritual ideals?" Only two responded affirmatively. It is often a cop-out when a father says, "It is not the quantity of my time that counts, but the quality." A child needs time with his father. Lots of it! There is no known substitute for the physical presence of a loving father in the home. Because so many children see their fathers as busy or angry, they are afraid to ask for his special attention.

It is our experience that dads do deeply love their children. They do not want a barrier of fear to replace the healthy respect that should exist. They can earn this respect by teaching the child how much they value him. That means they must discard their unreasonable specifications and accept the child as he is. It requires time with the child, exploring his interests and abilities and then letting him know the importance of these, even if they differ from dad's.

Another way dads can value their children is by truly valuing their children's mother. In one family the children were consistently rude to their mother. A friend of their daughter was puzzled by this since she saw the parent being kind and loving. One day this friend was in that house for an extended time. Later she explained her perceptions to her own mother. "I know now why those kids treat their mother so badly. You should hear how their dad talks to her!"

RESPECT.   It has already been said that many parents see their children as extensions of themselves or as an inconvenience. They need to recognize each child as a unique and valuable individual. The parent is privileged to guide his potential toward the goal God had in mind for the child.

When the father truly acknowledges the value of a child, he will respect that child. Respect does not set the child above the father or, even in some ways, does it see him, as a child, having equality with the dad. It looks within the child and by faith, beyond, seeing his potential.

Resect is an inner quality and is shown by one's attitude and manner. When a child wants to talk, he needs to be heard with the intent listening of the heart as well as the mind. He needs to have a listener, within reason, at the time his ideas or problems arise. A child, for example, may come home bubbling with excitement about school or boiling with some injustice. He needs someone then to hear, care and validate his success or control his anger. If he waits too long, the memories fade, the feelings quiet down, and it seems pointless to him to remember. It must be said in fairness, however, that everyone need not jump to attention at a child's every word. Children can and must wait their turn to speak and consider the other demands on the father's time. They will, in fact, accept this if the father sincerely cares and honestly listens and responds when they *do* speak.

Respect also includes sensing the child's needs and helping him to meet those appropriately. It does not permit ignoring or discounting the child's feelings and problems, nor does it magnify them. Respect does not rescue the child from a hard job or consequences of mis-behavior. Respecting a child says, "I know that is hard to do (or take), but I know you can do it." Of course that presumes the parent does know he can!

Complimenting the child on specific qualities in his character or efforts also shows respect. So does the expressed confidence in his ability to make good choices and the display of respect for one's self, as a father.

4. **LAUGHTER.** Life, like our book, gets very heavy at times! During times of stress, a good laugh may relieve tension and permit resolution of the problems. A father who takes himself too seriously is often ridiculed by his children. Fathers need, however, to exercise good judgement regarding the time for humor or seriousness. A

father who can laugh at himself, is likely to create a climate that is comfortable for a child. He may even laugh with his wife or child when they can see the humor. It is infuriating, however, to be laughed at when one is truly upset.

There are two kinds of laughter, the wholesome, delightful type and the derisive or sarcastic kind. The latter is usually mixed with hostility and creates both confusion and helplessness in response. Some families and individuals hide their honest emotions under a veneer of fun that is frequently a lie.

Being able to play together, share jokes and mistakes and laugh together appropriately, will help families stay together. Fathers can set the tone for such good humor!

PRAYER. Dr. Ketterman shares this from her childhood:

> As a family, we gathered every morning around a big circle in our living room. No matter how busy he was or who was visiting, dad read from the Bible. He preached no sermons, never used the Bible to point out our "sins," but his absolute faith in its wisdom never wavered. It showed in his face and voice and was a rock I learned to rest on. He prayed simply, about matters that concerned me—and each of us. This became a tradition and a priceless one. Even more meaningful, however, were dad's private prayers. I vividly recall getting up late one night for a drink of water. The house was lighted only by the moon as I tiptoed to the kitchen. I felt, rather than saw at first, my big, strong daddy, kneeling humbly by the kitchen chair, silently pouring out his own deep needs to the Heavenly Father. I knew then, rather than believed, that God was real and that He must be very big indeed if my strong daddy needed Him. Even now, I can't imagine how I could have rebelled against such a father.

A ROLE MODEL. Today, even adults are struggling deeply with role models. Most of the old concepts that identified maleness and femaleness have been taken away by a new logic. How very confusing it must be to a child.

There *is* a difference between men and women. Twenty years ago, to make that simple statement would have drawn laughter from any group. Today it raises the ludicrous accusation of sexism. We are in a new process of stumbling over the terms *chairperson, his* and *her*, and *committee person*. In 1978, the United States armed forces directed that its questionnaires may not inquire into a person's sex, marital status, ethnic origin, age, and much other statistical information formerly used by the government and employers. This unisexual trend takes away from a child the means by which he identifies the qualities of maleness and femaleness.

The father is the child's first role model of God. God is not a psychological extension of a child's imagination, as humanists have argued. The child's view of God will be distorted if his dad does not exemplify godly qualities.

Both sons and daughters learn about manliness from their fathers. The type of man a son becomes and the type of husband a daughter marries will be strongly influenced by their perception of their father.

A man's treatment of his wife becomes a pattern for both sons and daughters. Boys learn how to be good husbands and daughters learn what to expect from their mates by their dad's example. A father whose attitudes and actions in his marriage are confused and inconsistent is a role model of unhappy marriage for his children.

The father provides the role model for value systems. In these crucial days of competition for the child's attention, it is imperative that fathers provide positive values. Communications experts say that the average person sees between twelve hundred and eighteen hundred advertisements a day; not always consciously perceived, but passing the eye on the way to school, on the pages turned in magazines and newspapers, on the television, and almost everywhere. In the course of interviewing for this book, one of the authors spoke with an imprisoned Black Muslim. When asked about the influence of his father, he responded, "All I learned from my father was how to con people."

A boy inevitably becomes much like his father unless he rebels. In such a situation he may make mistakes opposite to his dad's, but equally problematic. A folk song written by Harry and Sandy Chapin poignantly expresses the former.

> My child arrived the other day; he came to the world
>   in the usual way.
> But there were planes to catch and bills to pay; he
>   learned to walk while I was away.
> And he was talkin' 'fore I knew it, and as he grew
>   he'd say,
> "I'm gonna be like you, Dad, you know I'm gonna be
>   like you."
> And the cat's in the cradle and the silver spoon,
>   Little boy blue and the man in the moon.
> "When you comin' home Dad?"
> "I don't know when, but
>   we'll get together then; you know we'll have
>   a good time then."
>
> My son turned ten—just the other day; he said,
>   "Thanks for the ball, Dad. Come on let's play.
>   Can you teach me to throw?"
> I said, "Not today. I got a lot to do."
> He said,
>   "That's okay." And he, he walked away, but
>   his smile never dimmed, it said,
> "I'm gonna be like him, yeah, you know I'm gonna
>   be like him."
> Well, he came from college just the other day; so
>   much like a man, I just had to say, "Son, I'm
>   proud of you, can you sit for a while?"
> He shook his head and he said with a smile,
>   "What I'd really like, Dad, is to borrow the
>   car keys. See you later. Can I have them please?"
> And the cat's in the cradle and the silver spoon,
>   Little boy blue and the man in the moon.
> "When you comin' home, son?"

"I don't know when, but
   we'll get together then; you know we'll have
   a good time then."

I've long since retired, my son's moved away;
   I called him up just the other day.
I said, "I'd like to see you if you don't mind."
   He said, "I'd love to, dad, if I can find
   the time.
"You see, my new job's a hassle and the kids have
   the flu,
"But, it's sure nice talkin' to you, dad,
   "It's sure been nice talkin' to you."
And as I hung up the phone, it occurred to me,
   he'd grown up just like me;
   My boy was just like me.
And the cat's in the cradle and the silver spoon,
   Little boy blue and the man in the moon.
"When you comin' home, son?"
"I don't know when, but
   we'll get together then,
   "Dad, we're gonna have a good time then."

Harry and Sandy Chapin

FAIR AND PROMPT DECISIONS FROM DAD.   Mothers and fathers often defer to one another in decisions regarding a child. Karen, for example, may ask her mother if she may have a new dress. Mother, not being certain, may say, "Go ask your father" or "It's okay with me if it is with your dad."

Karen next goes to dad saying, "Mom said it's okay for me to have a new dress, if you say so."

Father is left in a real predicament. If he says no, he is bad because mother at least has implied her assent. If he says yes, he runs the risk of seeming only to give in because of mom's statement. Karen is left more than a little guilty of manipulating both.

Father needs to determine what areas of family life he can delegate to the authority of his wife and what he needs to retain exclusively. This should be explained and maintained consistently. When such a plan is followed, there is little room for manipulation, the child has a clear response which avoids frustration, and the home functions more smoothly.

CONFUSED ROLE MODELS. It takes more than a man living within the same four walls to be a father. Some biological fathers never become functional fathers to their children. The problem is especially acute among professionals.

A pastor stands at the pulpit on Sunday morning preaching with an infallible Book in his hand. There is a sense in which, if he rightly divides the Word of Truth, he preaches an infallible message. When he properly preaches the Bible, the people are required by Scripture to obey. "Obey them that have the rule over you . . ." (Hebrews 13:17). That kind of authority is awesome.

Many pastors find it very difficult to adjust to the dual role of father and God's minister with a divine message. The minister walks out of the pulpit and into the home where he has a responsibility both as husband and father. Often he maintains a godlike image in the home and speaks with the same sense of authority as in the pulpit. He is unbending and authoritarian. The children find it confusing and difficult to distinguish between his dual role as pastor and father. Frequently, because of role confusion, the children have no functional father, only a pastor. They miss the warmth, humor, and love of a normal home.

The reverse may also be true. A child whose father is a minister may not have a functional pastor. The family relationship is the most intense social contact known to man. The intimacy of the home, which exaggerates all the flaws and shortcomings, often makes it difficult for a pastor to minister to his own family. The visible mistakes in his life make him an ineffective spiritual leader in the home. His children have heard him publicly plead for better homes while they know their own is not what it should be. Tragically, a congregation demands eighty to one hundred hours each week from a pastor, depriving the minister's children of the physical presence of their father.

The whole affair is uncomfortable for the child and without really realizing it, the child has been deprived of both a pastor and a father. Many pastors' children become rebellious. The absence of a father with whom they can clearly identify is frequently a contributing factor.

Dr. Ketterman reported that her oldest daughter often said during her teen years, "Mother, stop analyzing me." The same phenomenon often happens to corporate executives. When a man comes home, he needs to consciously shift gears and become a husband and a father rather than an ever-present-vocational-authority figure.

Mother's Influence on Dad

The confusion in today's cultural-social climate is not limited to men and children. Women, too, have been trapped in the confusion of roles and do not know just what they can expect from a husband.

Women who have not found in their husbands the strength on which they need to lean have bit by bit assumed more responsibility and almost unwillingly become dominating. They have destroyed, through their own well-intended efforts, the last vestiges of real strength their men ever had. Nagging mothers tend to produce passive sons. They learn to act only in response to habitual prodding. The wife of such a man is set up by his learned reactions to continue his mother's pattern, and the wife finally discovers this is the only way to get him to act. They drift into a pattern of abuse, resistance, and eventual warfare. Wives would do well to remember the words of Solomon, "A continual dropping in a very rainy day and a contentious woman are alike" (Proverbs 27:15).

One mother described this situation perfectly. She and her husband had a storybook romance and an idyllic marriage, marred—paradoxically—by the birth of their first and only child. She quit work to enjoy her baby girl, leaving the entire financial responsibility to her husband. They had no savings, and, when special needs arose, she would simply ask him for money. The anxious new father became angry and accused her of expecting too much. She, in turn, decided he was stingy, even selfish. As financial problems worsened, the wife took over the bookkeeping. Her irritation was not really hidden by her offer to help him. The husband grew quiet, became withdrawn and angry, hurt at this exposure of his inadequacy. Next, the wife found he was too busy to repair household items. Her nagging served only to increase his resentment, so she took over the repairs. She continued to take over wherever he abdicated, until nothing was left but bitterness. They were divorced, and the mother efficiently raised her child alone. She never remarried. Her daughter, however, in search of the missing father, became overly involved with a man and bore his child, like her mother, alone.

Wives, flowing with the tide of the times, have also excluded fathers from the process of bearing a child. Mothers, until very recently, routinely went alone to the obstetrician for their prenatal care while the expectant father was at work. Television graphically portrays the concept of a nervous, bumbling, almost idiotic husband who could scarcely get his poised young wife to the hospital. A new father could see his baby, clean and primly tucked into its sterile bassinet, only through a glass. Mother carried the infant home to its disinfected nursery and took it to the pediatrician. Except for extreme circumstances, dad was not needed by the child except to pay the bills and, much later, offer a stiffly groomed arm to his daughter for her wedding march.

Mothers are typically softhearted. When a dad does discipline a child, he probably will do so in a way quite different from her. Not wanting to hear a child cry or feel hurt, she may urge the father to be easier or she may later comfort the child. The message this signals to the child is that his father really is cruel, and only mother properly loves him. The father infers that he can do nothing right, and he resents the interference. Not only do mothers criticize fathers' discipline, but they also find fault with many other traits about him. When this is done in the presence of children, they inevitably lose respect for their father and even for the critical mother!

One mother was especially severe in her habitual criticism of her husband. She spoke of him as an ignorant, incapable person who was hopelessly inadequate. Often she expanded her faultfinding to a sweeping indictment against all men. Her son, hearing these comments regularly, believed his mother. He, too, saw his dad as an offensive, obnoxious person. In order to avoid being cast into such a mold, he carefully watched his mother, copying her every mannerism and speech. By adolescence, he realized that he was a homosexual. He had identified with his aggressive and hostile mother to gain her approval and to avoid becoming like his condemned father. It was not, in this case, that the man was actually so bad, but that the mother's opinion of him was biased.

In these examples, some positive differences might have been possible if the wives had taken an honest look at their habits of dominating their husbands. According to Dr. Ketterman there is great resistance: "In a recent lecture on the role of wives, I was roundly criticized and even ridiculed for holding to the biblical concept of submission. Despite such criticism, I see this concept as the only answer to much marital strife."

She continues: "Submission does, however, need to be accurately defined. The Latin root words make the English word more meaningful. They are *sub*, meaning 'down or under,' and *mitto*, meaning 'I send.' Submission, then, means that with my power of choice, I, as a woman, have the strength and wisdom to send my will under that of my husband. This is not a slavish, doormat concept based on helplessness or inferiority. It is a position of strength that is enhanced through encouraging and facilitating the growth of the husband as well as the wife."

Chapter 8
Cure for Rebellion

It may well be that the most painful human experience is for one member of a family to reject another, especially if one is a parent or a child! A range of emotions and questions runs painfully through the heart of a concerned parent who has a rebellious child—just as they have run through the life of a child to produce such rebellion. Every time a book or article comes out on such a topic, the troubled parents who read it suffer from anxiety, self-blame, guilt, self-analysis, and remorse. Chief among the plaguing questions is, "What can I do to bring back my child?"

It is one thing to intellectually isolate mistakes and think about reconstructing the broken relationships, but the actual undoing and redoing process is quite a different matter. There may be some children of parents who read this book who will not change; who, out of calloused bitterness, refuse reconciliation.

It would, however, be criminal to catalog a long list of failures by parents and children without some assurance that there is a way back. Children can be brought home. Relationships, ruptured for years, can be repaired. There is hope as long as the child is alive; families can be rebuilt. In fact, relationships can be stronger than ever if proper steps are taken. It is only helplessness and despair that are to be feared. When parents are willing to throw away the mask of false pride and risk reaching out with new tools of understanding, patience, and love, a plan can be made that will work. It takes time, commitment, sacrifice, and tenacity. But it is worth it!

171

Luke 15: 11-24

The biblical story of the prodigal son is as instructive as it is beautiful. At first glance, it seems merely a happy episode of a reunion between a wayward son and a concerned, waiting father. A more careful study, however, will show that, although the emphasis is on the joyous reunion, the broader backdrop of rebellion, patient parental concern, the long waiting and forever watching in vain are all resolved. There is the eventual return and reconciliation. The son is restored. The story, like life, is a process, not an isolated incident. The threads which run through the account and tie together the waiting for the wayward son are patience, faith, and time.

This chapter is devoted to practical, constructive steps that may be taken to restore family unity. They are built upon the foundation of biblical principals and common sense. After choosing the particular suggestions that fit your problems, you as parents of a rebellious child, are urged to decide to take action. The sooner you begin, the sooner your goal of the restoration of a loving relationship will be realized. Here are the steps:

① Acknowledge Parental Responsibility

Like it or not, you are primarily responsible for your child's behavior—good or bad. Mental or physiological abnormalities complicate your job as parents; so do cultural and social influences, peer pressure, and certain negative educational factors. But your influence is and always has been the greatest. To blame anyone else is only to deny or belittle your positive influence.

The first step you must be willing to take, if you would restore your relationship with your child, is to know and accept that his behavior and beliefs are fundamentally of your doing. Little can be accomplished until you reach that point. Many families focus the blame on the child, and by his resentment he becomes still more rebellious. By frankly and honestly sharing this blame, the *culprit* is joined by the *judge*. He no longer stands alone, condemned; they stand together. This acknowledgement, though it may appear insignificant and even simplistic, is profoundly important to changes.

Both parents must cooperate in this step. It is tempting for one parent to blame the other as well as for both to blame the child. To avoid further manipulation and lack of trust by the child, the parents' unity must be established. As they resolve their differences, unite, and accept their share of responsibility for the problems, the initiative to act in making positive changes is shifted to them from the rebellious child. Rebellion always involves a power struggle. By sharing in the blame, parents do away with most of the ammunition; the battle can stop and the reconstruction begin.

Every parent wants sincerely to be a good parent and to raise good children. So this first step of admitting some failure is intensely painful. For parents who may have a lifelong pattern of shifting responsibility to others, it may be nearly impossible to choose to accept this themselves. To suddenly admit such responsibility for a child's painful misbehavior may create immense guilt and depression. A father at just such a point shouted, "I have killed my own son!" His son had taken his life, but the father blamed himself and suffered overwhelming guilt and grief.

Guilt, alone, is not a solution. It can be destructive and, in its numbing effect, may even cause irrational behavior and complicate the problems endlessly. Guilt may cause the parent to assume too much responsibility and make him try to rescue the child rather than help him to grow through the experience. Guilt in its best sense, however, can be the pain that motivates one to deal with the problem and make the changes that will resolve it.

Forgiveness must occur along with the awareness of responsibility. Forgive yourself! To avoid unhealthy guilt and the mistakes that it will produce, you must find the strength of forgiveness. First, understand what mistakes you have made, then why you have made them. Almost always, though one's methods may be wrong, the motives have been right. Looking back over life, most parents will honestly say, "I did, each day, the very best I could, under the circumstances." By understanding, then, forgive yourself; learn from those mistakes; and find courage to form new and better ways.

A pastor once counseled a woman on several occasions about guilt over a sin she had committed. She had forsaken it and confessed it to God. But the feeling of guilt persisted. The pastor counseled with her several more times to no avail. Finally, in a desperate attempt to help her find peace, he asked the woman to stand before a mirror in the privacy of her home and say, "I forgive myself." That same afternoon she called his office and with tears of joy related that she was at last free from the sense of guilt.

Next, forgive your mate. It may well be that one parent is flagrantly guilty of wrongdoing, or the behavior of the wrongdoer may be very subtle so that no one honestly knows. Almost always it is a truly shared responsibility. Admitting one's own part, openly, honestly, and without accusing the other, can avoid further battles and set the pattern for honesty in dealing with the rebellious child later. The parents may need to confess to the child what they have discovered and include him in their decision to cooperate lovingly in the future. Such open sharing may free the child from a load of guilt he has carried for their disagreements. Many children assume the blame for parental disagreements.

Forgive your child. By understanding their own responsibility, parents may come to see that the problems of the child are partly their own. They may be aware that the child's rebellious behavior has meaning, that it has often been a response to their own behavior and was not begun in anger or with the intent to hurt them.

A friend on vacation was having a hard time with her preteen daughter. Nothing seemed to please her. She was petulant and disagreeable. The mother had just read a book on the harm of resentment in a relationship. Prayerfully and privately she listed all the things she resented about her child's attitudes and actions. One by one, she gave them up to the caring of the Heavenly Father. Unaware of her own inner changes, the mother saw a miraculous change in her daughter. Their vacation and their relationship were transformed.

It is important that child and parents alike *experience God's for-*

giveness. One teenage girl, caught in the act of shoplifting, said, "God must hate me!" How important to help her—and all of us who, like her, have gone astray—to see that God's love for her remains unchanged. He knows the anguish that both prompted and resulted from her act. He only wants us to look at Him, to see the love, acceptance, and restoration awaiting those who will see and receive them from Him.

Make Full Restitution for the Wrongs of the Past

It may be painful to admit and correct the wrongs of the past. Many of these wrongs can never be undone. To confess them as your offenses to your own child will begin a remarkable work of healing. It takes a strong, mature person to admit mistakes, and your child will experience a new respect for you as you express this to him. He has been more aware of your faults than you ever guessed—more even than you yourself were aware.

A mother of a thirteen-year-old son illustrates the need for restitution. This boy, since childhood, had been a dreamer. He was late for everything from getting up in the morning, to bedtime at night. He daydreamed in class, over homework, or raking leaves. His mother could foresee only failure for her only son if his behavior did not change. So she reminded him constantly with ever-growing irritation about his faults. It is clear that her chronic response was nagging and breeding resentment and rebellion. Their relationship was rapidly deteriorating into a constant battle with mutual pain and anger becoming habitual.

One day this mother realized what she had been doing, i.e., focusing almost entirely on the problems and rarely on the person of her son. With her newly broadened vision, she saw him as a gentle, sensitive young man who never hurt another person or an animal. He budgeted his money; he was always available to help a friend in any way he could. Suddenly, the problems slipped into perspective and became small when contrasted with his strengths.

This mother found the courage and the time to open her heart to her son. She confessed to him, with tears, the needless hurts she had inflicted on him and the mistakes she had made. She listed the newly recognized assets in him and let him know how much she valued him. Furthermore, she made a strong commitment to change and shared with her son that changing her habits of years would be hard. She admitted she would at times fail and asked his help and forbearance. It was a turning point in both their lives and undoubtedly prevented a serious rebellion by the son.

The two daughters of a pastor were taking piano lessons. Their parents had long dreamed of the day these girls could share in the ministry of their church through this musical talent. For years, the older girl had been the object of constant parental pressure to discipline herself to practice one hour every day. She wanted to play well but not to practice regularly. Rules, schedules, loss of privileges, all failed to make her practice. Teacher and parents alike seemed powerless.

After thirty years of teaching, the piano instructor finally retired. She wrote to this gifted girl a beautiful letter describing her potential and encouraging her to enroll in a music conservatory. She was highly complimentary. The pastor was greeted that evening by his daughter with letter in hand. She watched him read from start to finish, making sure he knew there was more on the back page. This letter, with its focus in her strength rather than her resistance, motivated her as nothing had ever done.

Both examples contain important elements needed to help a child. Nagging is problem-centered, while praise and encouragement focus on the positive potential in the child.

Neither time nor age need be a barrier in making restitution. It is never too late. A pastor counseled for some months with an engineer and his troubled wife. For over twenty years there had been conflict in their home because the beautiful and gifted wife felt she had never been accepted by her husband's parents. She had grown bitter and resentful toward them. At the pastor's suggestion, she called her mother-in-law, confessed her bitterness, and asked forgiveness. Almost immediately the marriage improved and the mother-in-law began to respond. It is almost impossible to stay angry with someone who loves us.

Restitution should become a habit applied as soon as possible after every misunderstanding. Restitution is a prevention for rebellion as well as a cure. The seventeen-year-old son of a pastor was going out one evening with a carful of youths to invite young people to the church. He had committed a minor offense before leaving, and his father was irritated by his actions. In the presence of his friends, his preacher father gave him a royal "chewing out" for his infraction. As he quietly drove out of the parking lot, his father suddenly became aware of the fact that he had embarrassed his son in front of his friends (the mother's disapproval shouted at him through her silence). Thinking and acting swiftly, the repentant father followed him in another car and motioned him to the curb. He met the perplexed son in front of his car and confessed that what he had done, as a father, was even worse than the son's misdeed. He admitted there was no justification for publicly embarrassing him. Father and son, standing in the glare of headlights on a dark street, became emotionally one as they sensed the warmth of forgiveness and restoration.

The child as well as the parent needs to make right his wrongs. After the child has time to experience healing through the new attitudes of his parents, he may be helped to make right his own misdeeds. It may take months or years of maturing before he has the strength of character to admit and correct his wrongdoings.

One young man, as a college junior, finally was able to admit several costly pranks he had played on neighbors while in high school. He paid for the price of the repairs his mischief had made necessary.

Restoring your child means loving and accepting him as he is. It is easy to love a child who acknowledges his rebellion, repents, cuts his hair and dresses to please you, and returns to church and family prayers; but, rebellious children need love before any of this takes place. There is no technique, no science, or advice that is a substitute for genuine, unconditional love. It is urgently important to accept and love them just as they are—with greasy, stringy hair; reddened, vacant eyes; and dirty, smelly bodies.

One young man, caught in a web of sin and disobedience, listened in boredom as his mother repeated to him an old, old story of how much God loved him and how disappointed God was in his behavior. The stored anger and pain of years erupted with the exclamation, "Mother, you've told me all my life that God loves me. I know that! What I want is to hear you say you love me—exactly as I am!" That is the cry of every rebellious teen or adult. "Please, somebody love me! Someone I can see and feel with my senses. Then, maybe I can learn to believe God loves me—a God I can't see with my eyes or touch with my hands." Parents often act as if it were immoral to love the child while he is rebellious. The reverse is actually true.

Contracts and Commitment to Change

Out of the admission of mistakes, the acceptance of responsibility, and making right the wrongs, hopefully, parents will spell out some specific changes that need to be made. Perhaps you have worried too much and have overreacted. You may have lectured or nagged. You may have controlled or dominated your child's life rather than guiding and teaching him a sense of responsibility and wisdom of his own. Perhaps you were too busy and unwillingly neglected his emotional and personal needs. Maybe you abdicated as a parent almost entirely and allowed your child to grow up alone or literally with only one parent.

You can change whatever your mistake or sin. It is comforting and exciting to know *you can change.* Besides the awareness of what needs changing, you need to make a definite decision to do so. It is important that this decision be clearly stated, i.e., "I will change the way I list my priorities." Any statement phrased like "I have to" or "I know I ought to" or "I plan to" simply will not produce change. However, definitive statements like, "Here's what I will do, and this is the help I will need," are quite surely the hallmarks of a successful reformation.

Be content with little changes at first. This applies to both you and your child. Habits are deeply engraved in our brains and are slow to be erased and rebuilt in new patterns. Good and permanent changes take place slowly.

Children need to see to believe! During the healing of rebellion, the child needs to see the consistency of the parents' changes. A parent who had an explosive temper, for example, may commit himself to patience and reasoning. Though he may succeed at this for six weeks, one explosion can so frighten a child conditioned to anger, that he will forget the past six weeks in recalling the prior sixteen years. Nevertheless, if the parent at once admits his failure and immediately gets back in control, he can still win.

Demonstrate Genuine and Lasting Personal Changes

Children are far more perceptive than we give them credit for. It is not infrequent that parents have made a series of well-meaning but false starts in reshaping the relationship between parent and child. A wary child may need time to test the parents' honesty in admitting mistakes. He may suspect them of playing psychological games to trap him when rebellion has reached a deep level of intensity. Parents must decide if there is time to live out the changes of their admitted mistakes. The risk of overdosing or aggression that could result in suicide or a serious accident is a very real danger in the youth culture of today.

A child needs to sense that there have been real changes in the personal spiritual life of the parent. Spiritual continuity and integrity must be evident. Real spiritual changes are internal, but their reality is easily seen. "But the fruit of the Spirit is love, joy, peace, longsuffering, gentleness, goodness, faith, meekness, temperance . . ." (Galatians 5:22, 23). Any child will recognize those qualities, given sufficient time to observe.

A child, during the time of healing, needs to see consistency in the parent. Erratic shifts of attitude toward a child, alternating between promises of a new beginning and sudden outbursts of anger, are unconvincing. A parent who will allow himself to be controlled by

God's spirit can provide the emotional support of predictable and concerned behavior.

Communications Corrections

Every parent of a rebellious child must believe that it is never too late for a reconciliation. Though personalities are formed early and temperaments may be largely hereditary, changes in behavior and attitudes can be brought about at any time. These changes, however, do not just happen. They take place because someone cares enough to work for them. The major tool that affects this change between parents and children is good communication.

Communication is the giving and receiving of information. This requires the careful translation of one's thoughts into words that can be understood by the other. It demands checking out by questions what the other one has heard. Words must be accompanied by a tone of voice, facial expression, and other physical mannerisms that convey the same meaning if real communication is taking place.

Listen. Sending out ever-so-clear messages, however, is not communication unless they are heard by someone. Listen to your child, then, as well as talk to him! This demands an open and unbiased mind that is willing to hear. In many heated family quarrels, each one is so busy thinking of what he plans to say next to get his point across, that no one really hears what is being said.

The most important listening is done, not with the ears, but with the heart. The caring heart will see the trembling lips and uncontrollably watery eyes, and not simply hear the angry voice. True caring will discover the heart of real communication. It is there—and then—that understanding springs forth, forgiveness takes place, and healing occurs.

An angry family sat together in a counselor's office. Father and daughter especially showed irritation that deepened into a dialogue of staccato comments which hurt and lashed back. Strangely incongruous, however, was a look of deep pain in the eyes of the father. A quiet comment from the counselor acknowledging the man's torment gently removed the armor of anger, first from the dad and soon from the daughter. It took only the slightest encouragement, and they were in one another's arms, weeping away the icy barrier of many years.

In a serious effort to learn to listen to his ten-year-old son, a father took the boy out to lunch. During a man-to-man conversation, the concerned dad put two questions to him. He asked first, "If you could change one thing about your father, what would it be?" His son squirmed in some embarrassment, but he quickly knew the answer. "I wish you weren't gone from home so much," he said wistfully. The father now felt discomfort as his son's comment hit its target squarely.

The second question was even more painful: "If it were absolutely necessary for you to have another father, whom would you choose?" The father was searching in the reply for the qualities his son needed from him. The boy pondered for some time before naming a man of his father's age, a close friend of the family. This man was noted for his interest in young children. The father knew what he must do to save his relationship with his son.

The timing of good communication is a critical factor. Things said in the heat of anger or the depths of despair are often not true and can widen the gulf between people. Anger generates anger, and despair is contagious. It is best to be alone during a time of intense feeling or to attempt to remain still until the mind takes control over the feelings. Then, talking with calmness about the problem and those feelings can bring about solutions and understanding.

As one learns to recognize feelings, it is possible to express them early, before they build up and explode beyond control. When parent or child will risk sharing hurts and concerns with honesty and openness, rather than masking them with anger or indifference, further pain can be avoided and reconciliation will take place.

Good communication involves few words. Parents are very likely to deliver lengthy lectures, some of them repeated so often they are memorized by their child. One boy recently said, "I know all my parents' lectures by heart. I don't even listen to them anymore!" Despite his impudence, this teenager was honest, and he spoke for many whose parents, like his, miss the mark of their best intentions.

Good communicators accept one another's feelings. Feelings are not wrong, but the way they are used may be very wrong. One father found his high-school daughter listening to a radio broadcast of a basketball tournament in which her classmates were playing. She was excitedly yelling for her team as she listened to every bit of action. The father found this to be foolish and soundly berated her for acting silly. He so commonly scolded her that she learned to suppress most of her emotions and later suffered repeated, serious, mental breakdowns.

While feelings give life richness and vibrancy, they must be expressed with control and honesty. Men often believe it is unmasculine to cry or admit fear, so they cover their vulnerable feelings with gruffness. Women, on the other hand, are sometimes taught to use their feelings. Many women cover their anger with tears—those "soggy weapons" designed to manipulate their families. Confusion dominates when such habits are the mode of communication.

A group of teenage girls were airing their gripes about their parents. The group leader asked them if they had ever tried to discuss these problems and their irritation directly with their parents. An instant and united response indicated that, to the girls, not one would dare to be so open with her feelings for mom or dad. How tragic for parents not to risk hearing things that admittedly could hurt, while their children retreat in silent anger. Each becomes isolated from the other.

There are three simple steps to use in dealing with unpleasant feelings between people. First, name the feeling; specify it exactly. "I am irritated." "I am angry!" "I am enraged!" By choosing the precise word, one's mind is activated, and it begins to gain control over the feeling. *Second, define why you feel as you do.* In the event surrounding your feeling, what specifically triggered that emotion. *Third, what will you decide to do about that situation?* By the time you have answered this question honestly, you will have the solution not just to the feeling, but to the pattern of events that has habitually produced the unhappiness. It is important that you make these steps very personal and not blame the other person for your feelings.

Discipline

It is necessary to define the word *discipline* to have a foundation on which to build one's understanding. It comes from a Latin word *discipulus* meaning, in its various forms, "to become acquainted with" or "to learn." *Disciples* are learners. Discipline may be well intentioned, but it turns into punishment unless some learning is involved. And the latter often results in rebellion rather than maturing.

Effective discipline involves three components: (1) clearly defined expectations or policies; (2) enforcement of these policies through an agreed upon process; (3) consistency and follow-through. In earlier childhood this entire process is up to the parents. By adolescence, however, it is important for the child to be included in such planning. This gives parents a prime opportunity to know their child's ways of thinking and show him respect for his ideas and feelings. Input from the child enables parents to be fair and considerate.

Policies vary from one family to another. They are related to traditions and individual family values. But, broadly, they must include daily time schedules, curfews, household and personal responsibilities, finances, and consideration and regard for each other as family members. It is vital that these policies not become an avenue in which to battle against each other.

The goal of parental discipline is self-discipline. Whatever the expectations and methods of discipline, the results must be evaluated. Is the youth more aware of his misbehavior, sorry for it, and willing to change? Is his attitude positive and his behavior changing for the better? Or, is he sullen, increasingly uncooperative, waiting behind thickening walls of defiance to become big and strong enough to openly rebel? Discipline that produces fear or defiance is doomed to failure.

What means of discipline will work for a teenager? Rarely indeed is this means physical. While corporal punishment may be lifesaving for a young child, it becomes an insult to most teenagers. The punishment needs to be fair and meaningful to the child—not just a release of frustration by the parent. It should be commensurate with the "crime" and when possible should be restricted to the day or week of the misdeed. Prolonged or excessive punishment may leave parents with no resources for later wrongdoing and certainly makes it hard to remember to follow through.

Some methods that most teenagers respect and even expect are: being grounded; forfeiting their allowance; repairing or making right the wrong; or being deprived of a privilege. Correction may even take place through encouragement and honest praise for doing the good or right thing. It is most important that parents neither accuse their child hastily nor protect him blindly. Many children are rescued from the natural consequences of their misdeeds by over-protective parents. Children soon learn to profess repentance or prey upon the parents' sympathy in ways that get them off the hook. These young people learn to manipulate in dishonest ways that result in anxiety and guilt.

Basic agreement between parents is imperative in good discipline. Parents must stick together in formulating policies and consequences and especially in the consistent follow-through of these. Commonly, one parent is more softhearted than the other. This may afford a fine balance in parenting; or, it may create confusion and eliminate good discipline.

When a mother, for example, is a gentle, easygoing parent, she may let a child get by with a misdeed and even conspire not to tell the father. She may modify its consequence to make it easier, or, by such a subtle thing as a pained expression, she may imply that dad is too harsh.

A father, understandably, resents this attitude that makes him always the "bad guy." He worries about the dangers of mother's leniency and tends to double his own efforts at discipline. He may transfer his irritation at his wife, whom he really loves, to their children. This results in a surcharge of anger and harshness in punishment. Mother completes the vicious cycle by feeling so very sorry for the poor child, rescues him even more, and on it goes. A totally destructive method! Moms and dads must work through their basic differences until they can honestly pull together with each other and for their children.

When a child is actively rebellious, it is of utmost importance to know if this is the result of too much punishment, too little discipline, or inconsistency. If the parents have been rigid and unfair in their approach, reconciliation cannot come about by intensifying the same mistakes. Instead, with open minds, this family needs to confer honestly about what is basically bearable for both and build from this foundation. If the parents have expected too little and have failed to set the limits so necessary to protect their child, they need to plan with their child ways to correct this. Agreeing upon policies that are both fair and purposeful will probably enlist the cooperation of the child and begin the end of his rebellion. Consequences, too, need to involve input by the "rebel" if he is to be expected to help in changing things. Inconsistency is hard to change because it results from understandable energy drains by other life demands. When there is trouble in the home, the priorities must be sorted out so enough time and energy can be focused on the problem to effect the cure.

Good discipline involves trust and respect. In the process of developing rebellion, there is a mutual loss of trust and respect between parent and child. This must be earned back if the cure is to take permanently. Since habits become automatic and hard to break, it is very hard to determine if early improvements are real and lasting. Trusting too much may invite backsliding. Too little trust is certain to result in discouragement. The best answer for this lies simply in being honest. A comment such as, "I really want to trust you to be honest with me, but it's easy to remember when you weren't. Please forgive me when, for a time, I check you out." When this is said out of love and honesty, it can be tolerated. Remember to expect the best from your child as well as yourself.

What Kind of Help Is Needed to Cure Rebellion?

A child who has been deeply hurt, is angry, or drug addicted, may be incapable of making wise choices or cooperating in any way with his parents. Help from sources other than the family may be the only answer for these young people. When spiritual needs or issues are involved, a pastor is invaluable. But sometimes there are physical, mental, or emotional issues at stake that demand the aid of a skilled mental health professional. In many cases, especially involving drug addiction or suicidal risks, hospital care may be necessary to save life and begin the long road back to mental health.

Parents commonly dread this separation and reject the only logical means of help because of an unnecessary sense of shame or guilt. First you need a clinical therapist whom you can trust for spiritual, as well as mental, health. The advice of a trusted family physician, minister, or friend can help in this first step. Heartbreaking as it is, you must marshal your courage, decide to trust this person and essentially turn over to him the care of your child. In working with a great many institutionalized youths, it was discovered that those who made the most complete and rapid recoveries, were those whose parents found the strength to do this.

One girl of fourteen, after some three years of drug involvement, truancy, and open rebellion, ended her disaster course in a hospital. She was asked what might have stopped her destructive habits sooner. After serious consideration, she conjectured, "Maybe no one could have stopped me. I probably had to find out for myself. But I think if my parents or anyone had ever said, 'Hey Sue, you're not yourself anymore,' I might have stopped to think." Her parents had been unable to face up to the problem and had simply denied it though she openly flaunted her drug habit, secretly hoping they would notice and help her stop. It took an overdose and a near death before they finally heard her.

When professional help is necessary, great care is needed in selecting a counselor, not only for the trust required in working together, but also for the assurance of being properly guided. One young woman entered on a disaster course of prostitution when her desperate plea for help brought only, "Just pray about it," from a minister. On the other extreme are the most skilled therapists who deny spiritual values and treat the Bible as if it were a handbook for witch doctors.

A pastor referred a parishioner to a clinical psychologist. He had not realized the counselor totally ignored the Bible. The troubled client was obsessed with pornography and perverted sexual thoughts and actions. This tormented man was told that the problem was not with him but his puritanical values, and that he was really angry with God. He was directed to, with a pillow, symbolically beat and shout out his anger against the loving Heavenly Father. God certainly was not threatened by this poor man's anger, but since his problem and that solution missed reality so far, he could hardly find peace. It took the pastor years to undo the spiritual as well as psychological damage that was done in a few weeks.

Spiritual Help for Rebellion

This aspect of the cure for rebellion was placed last because it is so vitally important. Man is the only one of God's creatures who has a spiritual nature. Since it is unique to mankind, we must maintain its foundational significance if personal, as well as family, wholeness is to be achieved.

Thousands of years ago, God inspired Moses to write in Deuteronomy 6:7, "And thou shalt teach them [God's commandments] diligently unto thy children, and shalt talk of them when thou sittest in thine house, and when thou walkest by the way, and when thou liest down, and when thou risest up." God obviously planned for parents to communicate Him and His way of life to their own children. The abdication of parental responsibility for this teaching to any other resource is offering children the second best.

The Bible gives a sure promise, on the other hand, to parents who obey God. "Train up a child in the way he should go; and when he is old, he will not depart from it" (Proverbs 22:6). In fact, Solomon in his God-given wisdom said that discipline is an evidence of love for a child: "He that loveth him chasteneth him betimes" (Proverbs 13:24). Webster defines *chasten* thus: "To punish in order to correct or make better," and gives as the Latin root words *castus* meaning "pure" and *agere* meaning "to lead." To chasten, then, is to lead a child to purity. This clarifies the positiveness of the biblical concepts as being loving, not harsh or rigid. Good psychology validates positive discipline and so does good scriptural understanding.

Ask for and listen to God's direct guidance. Many people today, in reaching out to human resources for guidance and help (and that we need to do), may forget that God Himself will guide them in times of crisis. We believe that God deeply loves each of His creatures and has provided His Spirit especially to touch their every need and hurt. One mother related this experience:

> Her youngest child was just starting to date and was exuberant in the newfound hope that at fifteen she just might not have to face spinsterhood. On the occasion of her first date, she returned later than her parents expected. She alleged she had not been told exactly when to be in. The following evening, with a well-defined and agreed-upon curfew, she again came home quite late.
>
> Her mother waited anxiously with anger displacing concern, feeling hurt and confused that her loving child could so suddenly seem calloused to her worries. Fortunately, the anger, with all the harsh comments it prompted in her thoughts, had time to turn the mother again to thoughtfulness. Just how should this crisis be handled? The wrong approach could start a misunderstanding that so quickly could turn love to rebellion. Focusing her feelings and thoughts, the mother prayed, "Jesus, You've said You would always be with us. If You were standing here, what would You do? What would You say to my child?" No mystical vision or voice was experienced, but this troubled mother suddenly remembered a scene when her daughter was three. It was Christmas and loving relatives had showered the little girl with exciting toys—too many to use or even comprehend all at once. She had become frantic in her efforts to enjoy them.
>
> When Nancy finally came home, she nervously went to her mother, starting needless excuses. Her mother tenderly cradled the young head in her arm, while she related this wonderful scene from her childhood. She gently tucked Nancy in bed.
>
> With no more reaction, the very next day, this mother overheard the following comments during her child's telephone conversation: "No, Bill. I can't stay out that late. No! I have to be in by 11:00 o'clock. No, in the house!"

A potential rebellion was avoided because this mother remembered God's promise to guide her and to be her wisdom.

God has established His laws and commands. He does not set these aside to intervene in a different way. He does work through these laws and through the instinctive awarenesses with which He created us. It is our responsibility, as His children, to learn these laws and to work in cooperation with Him through them.

A Christian counselor verified the fact of God's wisdom being made a tool for healing in a counseling session. A woman went to his office for help with problems resulting from a brutal rape by her father, which had occurred sometime previously. He was drunk and ruthlessly assaulted her and left her alone. She later told her mother what had transpired but was met only with anger and harsh accusations. The young woman had locked away this painful event until circumstances brought it all back. She desperately wanted help, but it was evident that the s ame and sense of being "dirty" held her captive. She could not talk it out, could not believe the acceptance and concern of the counselor. Every skill of this experienced person failed to penetrate the barriers this event had erected through the years that had passed.

But this counselor knew another resource. He inwardly prayed for the love and guidance of the Heavenly Father, to touch the pain he could not reach. He asked the woman if she believed in Jesus. She sadly nodded in assent, obviously feeling no better. She was asked next, "Will you, in your imagination, picture Jesus entering into the room where your rape took place? What do you think He would do?" It was evident that Jesus did indeed stand by her side and reach out His hand to pull her up to His loving embrace. The tears, frozen by her tragedy, melted; and she wept. Her crying continued for some time as she sensed His comfort, felt His healing, and accepted His understanding of those who had so cruelly wronged her. She was miraculously enabled to forgive her parents. Her appearance was transformed. Her manner was open and friendly as she left to live out in new relationships the healing she had experienced.

Parents must live their faith if the child is to believe. Even born-again Christians often do not know how to experience such specific guidance. Many parents have not learned to pray at all. When parents begin to grow spiritually or experience a spiritual birth, the change in their lives may be confusing to children. The changes in their values and life-style may slip back to old patterns at times, as is the manner of human beings. If children are to believe parents' changes are real, and not just a psychological manipulation, they must have solid evidence. Integrity and continuity must be apparent in a new manner of life. Spiritual changes are internal, but their realness is externally seen. This must be a daily way of life over a span of time. Does this sound superhuman? It is! Only by God's own power can such a life be achieved. "But the fruit of the Spirit is love, joy, peace, longsuffering, gentleness, goodness, faith, meekness, temperance . . ." (Galatians 5:22, 23). Fruit grows if the life of God's spirit is permitted and nourished within us.

Fathers are patterned after God's image. Early psychiatrists taught that God was nothing more than a magnification of one's father. They were entirely wrong, but they had happened onto a profound truth. Fathers were meant by God to be—to the impressionable child—a believable image of Himself. In Ephesians 6:4, fathers are told, "Provoke not your children to wrath [rebellion]: but bring them up in the nurture and admonition of the Lord."

In the course of interviewing one hundred young people, each was asked if his father personally taught him on a one-to-one basis what he believed and wanted the child to believe. Only 30 percent responded affirmatively.[1] Parents have, perhaps without realizing it, abdicated their authority as spiritual teachers of their children, to churches, books, or a vague someone else. This can only result in a spiritual vaccum within children's lives.

This vacuum will be filled. Our survey asked young people, "Who has had the most influence in causing you to question the values and theology of your father, teachers or friends?" All but fourteen answered, "Friends." This clearly means that when you, the parents, neglect to teach your child directly, even the example you live or the indirect teaching you do, is not enough. Dangerously, those in your child's relationships who have the least wisdom and maturity are most strongly shaping his beliefs. You dare not abdicate!

The picture of the father as the strong and protective person in a child's life is fading fast. Children's books, TV, and the facts of all too many families' lives add up instead to the sum of fathers' stupidity, bungling, or indifference.

That young people do correlate their dads with their concepts of God is confirmed by many experiences.

One teenager, with over twenty-five juvenile court hearings to his dubious credit, was at last sent to a mental-health clinic for an evaluation. As he was tested and interviewed minutely, the smart boy came through looking amazingly sound. He had the right answers to every question. Finally, someone asked, "Jim, what is your concept of God?" Again, Jim had a ready answer, but this one gave the clue so needed to understand and help him. "God," replied Jim, "is someone who loves you so much, He gets you out of all your difficulties!" Further questioning, then, revealed that Jim's dad, a traveling man, had consistently paid the fines and taken away the punishment that would have helpfully taught his son that crime doesn't pay. Jim had stayed a naughty little boy who never had to grow up and face the consequences of his actions. His father had indeed gotten him out of all his difficulties, only to create bigger ones.

Parents need the help of a Christ-centered church. The local church (a fellowship of believers) is clearly ordained by the Bible to strengthen Christians and to spread the Good News. *But the church alone cannot raise a child.* Another question our survey asked was, "What single person in your life has had the greatest influence in determining what you believe and the way you behave?" Sixty-six percent named the parents and the vast majority stipulated the father as the principal influence.

Families that pray together stay together. Just how prayer works is hard to say, but it does work. In fact, perhaps we needn't ask. Praying together can certainly stop power struggles. By submitting one's needs to the greatest Authority, it becomes irrelevant to discuss further who is right or who gets his way. Prayer must be expressed in love if it is to be effective. Hence praying will result in love's growth and expression in the life of the one who prays. And love is healing.

A national survey reveals that although one in three marriages ends in divorce, one in fifty-five fails where husband and wife attend church together. Even more startling was the revelation that only one in 1,018 marriages ends in divorce when the mates regularly pray together.

Exercise your faith. If you believe God will guide you and heal your rebellious child, you must evidence that faith. Children tend to become the good people you pray for them to be just as surely as they became the rebels you feared they might.

Both of the authors were fortunate in having parents who believed implicitly in our good behavior while we were in our teens. We agree that we were kept out of much wrongdoing because of our parents' faith in us—and their enduring prayers for us.

When everything possible is done, wait! There comes a time in dealing with a rebellious child, when nothing more can be done. If you have reached this place, with all the help you can get, let your child know you love him and accept him as he is. Tell him that you will wait for him to return—either physically or emotionally to you. Threats or pursuit beyond this will have diminishing returns and will even create a wider gap.

A youth minister in a southern city was threatened irrationally by the distressed father of a runaway son. Mistakenly, the dad believed the young pastor knew the hiding place of his child. He even threatened bodily harm to the pastor.

Fortunately, the young minister was physically powerful and not easily intimidated. He was also wise enough to help the frantic father to think about his son. He asked a pointed question: "Do you want your son home, or just his body?" Real restoration takes an inner change, not just an outward compliance.

In the fifteenth chapter of Luke's Gospel there are three meaningful stories related by Jesus. All three are concerned with the loss of something or someone precious—a sheep, a coin, a son. The shepherd searched through the wilderness until he found the stray and tenderly carried it back to the flock on his shoulders. The woman searched and swept her house diligently until she found the lost coin. But the father waited, searching the long road that led away from, but also back to, the home. His eyes must have watched patiently for so long, because they saw the dirty, ragged boy while he was still a vast distance away. In all three cases, the finding of the lost resulted in great joy and celebration.

Sometimes, when we have obeyed, trusted, and searched ever so diligently, all we can do is *wait*. Waiting with God will certainly bring results.

Teenage Survey: Questions and Answers

1. What grade level did you achieve in school?
   Average grade: 10.5
2. How many children are there in your family?
   Number of children: 3.8 average
3. What place in birth were you among children in your family?
   Average place: 2.5
4. How old was your father when you were born?
   Average age: 26.2 years
5. How old was your mother when you were born?
   Average age: 23.7 years
6. Have either of your parents been in full-time Christian service?
   Yes: 21%
   No: 79%
7. Have your parents been divorced?
   Yes: 28%
   No: 72%
8. At what age did you first seriously question the moral value system of your father?
   One hundred percent had seriously questioned the moral value system and the average age at which it occurred was 11.3 years.

9. If your parents were Christian, have you ever rejected any major part of their theology?
    Yes: 10%
    No: 90%

10. How long did you keep secret your doubts about your change of theology?
    Average time: three years

11. Have you ever seriously considered suicide?
    Yes: 34%
    No: 66%

12. At what age did you first seriously consider suicide?
    Average age: 13.6 years

13. Did you make specific plans to take your life?
    Yes: 32%
    No: 68%

14. Have you actually attempted suicide?
    Yes: 14%
    No: 86%

15. How many times have you attempted suicide?
    Three of the 14% who had actually attempted suicide had attempted more than once.

16. Did a specific book other than the Bible affect your thinking?
    Yes: 32%
    No: 68%

17. What was the title of the book that affected the way you think?
    No discernable pattern in responses.

18. How many books have you read in the past twelve months?
    Average number of books: 9.2

19. Did you have great respect for the intelligence of the ministers in your life?
    Yes: 77%
    No: 23%

20. Did you have great respect for the education of the ministers in your life?

Yes: 68%
No: 32%

21. Did you have great respect for the character of the ministers in your life?
    Yes: 67%
    No: 33%

22. Did the public-school system negatively influence the change in your attitudes toward your father's value system and theology?
    Yes: 68%
    No: 32%

23. Which of the following in the public-school system influenced your change of attitude the most?
    Friends: 43%
    Teachers: 5%
    Both: 24%
    Neither: 28%

24. What person in your life had the single greatest influence in shaping the way you believe and behave? The person may or may not be a member of your family. The influence may be either positive or negative.
    Father: 40%
    Mother: 26%
    Other: 34%
    (*Note:* 73% of those who responded "Other" had no father present in the home.)

25. What was your grade average in school?
    A: 18%
    B: 42%
    C: 31%
    D: 5%
    Below D: 4%

26. Have you ever attended a Christian school?
    Yes: 49%
    No: 51%

*27. Was the quality of teaching in the Christian school good?
      Yes: 94%
      No: 6%
*28. Were the rules in the Christian school too strict?
      Yes: 24%
      No: 76%
*29. Did the training in the Christian school enrich you spiritually?
      Yes: 70%
      No: 30%
*30. On balance, what effect did the Christian school have on your values?
      Positive influence: 70%
      Negative influence: 30%
31.   Do you wish you could change how you feel about your father's values and theology?
      Yes: 47%
      No: 53%
      (*Note:* Young people were generally unhappy that their moral values were upsetting to parents.)
32.   Do you believe that you or your parents are happier?
      Child happier: 52%
      Parent happier: 48%
33.   Did you lose the approval of your parents when your internal value system and theological changes were made known to them?
      Yes: 31%
      No: 69%
34.   Would you like your children to have the same values and theology that you have?
      Yes: 61%
      No: 39%
35.   Do you believe there is a God?
      Yes: 100%
      No: 0%

* These percentages were calculated from the 49% who had attended a Christian school.

36. Have you doubted there is a God?
    Yes: 48%
    No: 52%

37. Do you believe that the Bible is historically reliable?
    Yes: 98%
    No: 2%

38. Do you believe your children should learn the life principles of the Bible?
    Yes: 98%
    No: 2%

39. At what age did you first experiment with tobacco?
    Experimented: 74%
    Never experimented: 26%
    Average age: 10.3 years

40. At what age did you first experiment with marijuana?
    Experimented: 47%
    Never experimented: 53%
    Average age: 13.6 years

41. At what age did you first experiment with cocaine?
    Experimented: 14%
    Never experimented: 86%
    Average age: 15.8 years

42. At what age did you first experiment with alcohol?
    Experimented: 72%
    Never experimented: 28%
    Average age: 11.7 years

The following comparison was made between those who had attended Christian schools and those who attended only public schools.

	Christian School	*Public School*	*Total Survey*
Have experimented with tobacco	70%	77%	74%
Have experimented with marijuana	46%	49%	47%
Have experimented with cocaine	11%	18%	14%
Have experimented with alcohol	68%	77%	72%

43. Do you believe in the institution of marriage?
    Yes: 100%
    No: 0%

44. If you marry, will you deal with your children as your father did with you?
    Yes: 23%
    No: 77%

45. What major changes would you make in dealing with your children?
    The two most common answers given were:
    1. Better discipline
    2. Better communication
    (*Note:* No discernable pattern emerged except the above two responses.)

46. Are you sure that the changes you would make would work better than your father's?
    Yes: 48%
    No: 52%

47. If you had in your power the capacity to change one U.S. federal law, what would it be?
    Those desiring changes: 43%
    Those desiring no changes: 57%
    (*Note:* No discernable pattern emerged in laws wished changed. Survey revealed that young people interviewed are generally neither politically aware nor active.)

48. Do you believe in sex outside of marriage?
    Yes: 9%
    No: 91%

49. *Do your parents believe in sex outside of marriage?*
    Yes: 12%
    No: 88%

50. At what age did you first experiment sexually?
    Never experimented: 21%
    Experimented: 79%
    Average age: 12.6 years

51. Have you ever engaged in sexual intercourse?
     Yes: 36%
     No: 64%

The following comparison was made between those who had attended Christian schools and those who attended only public schools.

	Christian School	Public School	Total Survey
Have experimented sexually	78%	79%	79%
Sexual experiments include intercourse	31%	48%	36%

52. At what age did you first engage in sexual intercourse?
     Average age: 13.5 years

53. In your judgment what was the single most important factor in
     the rejection of the theology or values of your parents?
     1. Influence of friends: 24%
     2. Lack of communication: 12%
     3. Nature of discipline: 9%
     4. Absentee parents: 7%
     5. Hypocrisy in the home: 5%
     6. Other (no discernable pattern): 43%

54. Was it possible for you to confide in your father about your
     doubts regarding his values and theology?
     Yes: 50%
     No: 50%

55. Did your father make a practice of explaining his rules?
     Yes: 56%
     No: 44%

56. Did your father spank you?
     Yes: 90%
     No: 10%

57. Was your father generally angry when he spanked you?
     Yes: 42%
     No: 58%

58. When your father spanked you, which of the following did he use most frequently?
    Neutral object: 68%
    Hand: 22%
    Both: 9%

59. Did your father generally explain the spankings?
    Yes: 56%
    No: 44%

60. Was your father fair when he disciplined you?
    Yes: 51%
    No: 49%

61. Would you vote for a man for president who believed exactly as you do?
    Yes: 73%
    No: 27%

62. If you could change one thing about your father, what would it be?
    The two most common answers were:
    1. Father's temper
    2. Desire for more communication
    (*Note:* No discernable pattern emerged beyond these two responses.)

*63. Do you have any spiritual goals in life?
    Yes: 45%

*64. Do you have any vocational goals in life?
    Yes: 34%

*65. Do you have any educational goals in life?
    Yes: 7%

66. Did your father and mother fight orally or physically in your presence?
    Yes: 55%
    No: 45%

67. Did the inconsistencies in what your father taught and how he lived make it difficult for you?

* Fourteen percent had *no* goals in life. The young people surveyed were asked to choose which was the dominant goal in their life.

Yes: 55%
No: 45%

68. Did you have consistent family devotions in your home?
    Yes: 15%
    No: 85%

69. Did your father personally endeavor to teach you his moral and spiritual ideals?
    Yes: 30%
    No: 70%

70. Did you attend church consistently?
    Yes: 85%
    No: 15%

71. Did you look forward to being home with your family as a teenager or prefer being with your friends?
    Home: 44%
    Friends: 56%

72. Has time brought about any shift back toward views you formerly held before you became rebellious?
    Yes: 77%
    No: 23%

73. Does your mother practice the moral standards established by the father?
    Yes: 86%
    No: 14%

74. In your judgment who is or was the spiritual head of the home?
    Father: 67%
    Mother: 30%
    None: 3%

75. When disciplined, what form did it most often take?
    Grounding: 40%
    Spanking: 35%
    Depriving of privileges: 25%

76. When threatened with discipline, was it actually enforced?
    Yes: 68%
    No: 32%

77. Do your parents consistently engage in activities that are condemned from the pulpit?
    Yes: 28%
    No: 72%

78. Does it create conflict in you when your parents engage in activities that are condemned from the pulpit?
    Yes: 59%
    No: 41%
    (*Note:* These percentages were based on the 28% who responded yes in question 77.)

79 What were the standards of success your father established for himself?
    The two most common answers given were:
    1. Vocational achievement
    2. Rearing children properly
    (*Note:* No discernable pattern emerged except the above two responses.)

*80. Did your father most admire men with academic degrees?
    Yes: 9%

*81. Did your father most admire men with character?
    Yes: 38%

*82. Did your father most admire men with worldly influence?
    Yes: 13%

*83. Did your father most admire men with spiritual power?
    Yes: 40%

84. Was there tender affection expressed by your parents to each other in your presence?
    Yes: 76%
    No: 24%

85. Did you experience moral defeats that your father did not know about?
    Yes: 88%
    No: 12%

86. Did your parents speak out against other Christian leaders in

    * Young people were asked to *choose* what their fathers admired in other men.

your presence who might have been a bridge to bring you back from rebellion?

Yes: 44%

No: 56%

87. Do you feel you had any part in your father's ministry?

    Yes: 27%

    No: 73%

    (*Note:* This question was directed to those young people whose fathers were involved in salaried Christian service.)

88. Do you feel you had any part in your father's vocation?

    Yes: 6%

    No: 94%

    (*Note:* This question was directed to young people whose fathers held secular jobs.)

89. During your youth did you make a vital contribution to the cause of Christ (i.e., Christian service)?

    Yes: 34%

    No: 66%

90. Was your father wise and faithful with the family's money?

    Yes: 75%

    No: 25%

91. If your father was in full-time ministry, do you believe God was building his ministry or he was building his ministry?

    God was building ministry: 72%

    Father was building ministry: 28%

92. What areas of known inconsistency have you observed in your father's life?

    The two most common answers were:

    1. Hypocrisy

    2. Not keeping commitments made to children

    (*Note:* No discernable pattern emerged except the above two responses.)

93. What effect have friends had upon you in general?

    Negative: 44%

    Positive: 34%

    Neutral: 22%

94. Are there other questions that should be included in this survey?
    Yes: 32%
    No: 68%

95. Do you consider yourself rebellious?
    Yes: 56%
    No: 44%

96. Do you spend a significant amount of time with your parents?
    Yes: 55%
    No: 45%

97. Do you enjoy being with your parents?
    Yes: 60%
    No: 40%

98. Do you feel your parents' values (their view of what is important in life) are right or wrong?
    Right: 67%
    Wrong: 33%

99. Do you believe this survey is significant?
    Yes: 97%
    No: 3%

100. Do you believe this survey is fair?
    Yes: 100%
    No: 0%

101. Do you know Jesus as your Saviour?
    Yes: 90%
    No: 10%

Source Notes

Chapter 1

1. Jerry Rubin, *Growing Up at 37* (New York: Warner Books, 1976), p. 103.
2. *Ibid.*, p. 18.
3. "Saving the Family," *Newsweek* (May 15, 1978), p. 65.
4. *Ibid.*

Chapter 2

1. Arthur M. Schlesinger, Jr., *The Coming of the New Deal* (Cambridge, MA: Riverside Press, 1958), p. 373.
2. A. C. Nielsen, "What TV Does to Kids," *Newsweek* (Feb. 21, 1977).
3. Charles A. Reich, *The Greening of America* (New York: Bantam Books, Inc., 1971), p. 27.
4. *Ibid.*, p. 28.
5. Dr. James Dobson, *What Wives Wish Their Husbands Knew About Women* (Wheaton, IL: Tyndale House Pubs., 1975), p. 57.
6. James Hefley, "Artificial Imsemination: Sacred or Sinful," *Christian Life* (May, 1978).
7. Kenneth Keniston, "The Parent Gap," *Newsweek* (Sept. 22, 1975).
8. Sarane Boocock, "The Parent Gap," *Newsweek* (Sept. 22, 1975).
9. "The Parent Gap," *Newsweek* (Sept. 22, 1975).
10. Dr. Urie Bronfenbrenner, "The Origins of Alienation," *Scientific American* (Aug., 1974).

11. Alvin Toffler, *Future Shock* (New York: Bantam Books, Inc., 1970), p. 17.
12. Thomas Gordon, M.D., *P.E.T., Parent Effectiveness Training* (New York: New American Library, 1975), p. 276.
13. *Ibid.*, p. 194.
14. Teenage Survey, *see* p. 195.
15. Max I. Dimont, *The Jews, God and History* (New York: New American Library, 1962), p. 15.

Chapter 4

1. Teenage Survey, *see* p. 195.
2. *Ibid.*, p. 193.

Chapter 5

1. Arlene Skolnick, "The Myth of the Vulnerable Child," *Psychology Today* (Feb., 1978), p. 56.
2. A. D. Dennison, Jr., M.D., "God, I Can't Stand My Parents," *Christian Life* (Aug., 1970), p. 30.
3. William Glasser, M.D., *Schools Without Failure* (New York: Harper & Row Pubs., Inc., 1975), p. 22.
4. *Ibid.*, pp. 14–15.

Chapter 6

1. William Glasser, *Reality Therapy* (New York: Harper & Row Pubs., Inc., 1965), p. 42.
2. Ruth Carter Stapleton, "My Brother Billy, the Carter Brother Nobody Knows," *Woman's Day* (Oct. 23, 1978), p. 80.
3. *Ibid.*, p. 82.
4. Teenage Survey, *see* p. 195.

Chapter 7

1. "The Equal Rights Amendment," *Moody Monthly* (Nov., 1978).
2. Teenage Survey, *see* p. 195.

Chapter 8

1. Teenage Survey, *see* p. 201.
2. *Ibid.*, *see* p. 195.